THE MYSTICAL TAPE SERIES

REVEALING

——THE——

SEVEN-PRONG
PROCESS

Seminar/Tape Series

1978-79

HERB FITCH

Editor: Bill Skiles

To order additional copies of this book, contact:
Bookwhip
1-855-339-3589
https://www.bookwhip.com

CONTENTS

Tape 5

Tape 6

FOREWORD

BY
BY BILL SKILES

"And they shall be all taught of God. Every man therefore that hath heard, and hath learned of the Father, cometh unto me."
–John 6:45

To walk in the Kingdom of Heaven here and now, it is necessary to have the conscious awareness of Christ within, which must be renewed continuously throughout the day and night by frequent short meditations until that point of contact becomes a continuous conscious awareness of Being, even with eyes open.

This series of talks are the 1978 Mystical Tape Series by Herb Fitch which are intended to open Consciousness to the inner esoteric meaning of the scriptures in the Bible which have remained hidden for thousands of years to mortal thought. By having that listening ear within, by being receptive to what is revealed through these talks, the spiritual student will be led step by step to the secret place within where it is possible to hear the still small voice and be led by the inner Christ and be taught of God.

It is up to the spiritual student to study these talks and to put the principles into practice daily until such a time as that conscious contact with God becomes a continuous inner communion. And then, "At a moment ye think not, I am come," and Christ, that living Presence within, will lift you into the many mansions which have been prepared for you since before the world was.

Bill Skiles
Robbinsville, NC
03/26/12
Link : http://www.mysticalprinciples.com
(click the above link to go there.)

TAPE 1

LESSONS 1 - 4

Herb: Greetings of Love from the island of Kauai.

LESSON 1: YOUR DIVINE LIFE

This is a very precious moment. We are meeting new friends across the country, and on tape we are having our first reunion since the Kauai seminar last Easter. Then we studied the mystical tree of life, and for many of us, it was a very rewarding and exciting journey.

Now we meet again in a very special mystical series to prepare us for a still higher journey in consciousness, and hopefully most of us have realized by now that we are not here to seek human betterment or human benefit. For many of us that is not enough. We are instead seeking to find our permanent identity. We have seen through the decoy which limits us to temporary success in a temporary lifespan made of matter. That's not what we're looking for anymore. We can have all of that without studying The Infinite Way.

What we are trying to do in this message is to find a way to break through the crust of human consciousness into the pure experience of eternal life here, now, while seemingly moving on this earth. And so if you share these aspirations, you'll find something here for you; and we welcome you in oneness and

1

in love. Together, guided by pure divine truth, let us now move upward to fulfill our life purpose—to walk in the awakened consciousness of divinity.

Imagine now if you will, that in front of you stands a box, oh about three feet high; and we want to know what is in that box. Because when you understand the contents of that box, you will solve a mystery that has baffled man for more than one billion years. So let's give a name now to that box in front of you, and let's call it "Your Divine Life." Now let's look inside the box. We open "Your Divine Life" and inside we find another box. Now let's call this second box "Your Spirit." But wait; there's still another box within this box. Now let's call this third box "Your Soul." And so we have now three boxes, one within the other. They are "Your Divine Life", "Your Spirit" and "Your Soul." Remember that one unforgettable word: *Your* Divine Life, *Your* Spirit, *Your* Soul. And now, if you will, add one more important word: Your Divine Life *now*. Your Divine Spirit *now*. Your Divine Soul *now*. You have a more complete picture because whenever the Bible speaks to you of the Kingdom of God or the Kingdom of heaven, it is using mystical terminology. It is not speaking about a place. It is not speaking about geography. It is not speaking about some kind of destination that you will go to after you die. We're not going to make that error.

The Kingdom of God should always mean to you your Divine Life, your Spirit and your Soul; all three in one here and now. Here and now is important because when you become conscious *here* of your divine life *here*, then you have a divine consciousness, which is also called Christ consciousness. When you become conscious of your Spirit *here*, you have a spiritual consciousness. When you become conscious of your Soul *here*, you have a soul consciousness.

And so whenever the Bible speaks of the three heavens, remember it's speaking about your divine consciousness, which is the third heaven; your spiritual consciousness, which is the second heaven; and your soul consciousness, which is the first heaven. All three are the heavens of the Kingdom of God, and those are the three boxes that you have imagined in front of you, one within the other. They represent someone you should get to know. That someone is your permanent Self, your eternal Self. The Self that is as perfect now as God, which is also known as Christ, the eternal Son. That Self is your only self.

These three heavens—your Divine Life, Spirit and Soul—contain no sickness; no war; no cruelty; no hate; no disease, disaster, discord, destruction or death. Everything moves now here in your true Self, in perfect harmony, under perfect divine law. Your divine Self by its very nature is unopposed, unconditioned, unlimited, flawless, eternally self-sustaining.

But here's something quite strange. Look inside the third box and you'll find a fourth box. This box is called the "world mind." And this is where you find the human race. Every human being lives in mind consciousness, unaware of the three heavens above. In this fourth box of mind consciousness you find creatures of the flesh wandering; moving about; struggling in space and time; trying to remain alive; searching for peace, security, harmony, fulfillment; desperately wanting to survive. In this fourth box of mind consciousness you find good and evil, hate, love, war, peace, good health, bad health, birth, death, joy, sorrow, wealth, poverty, abundance, starvation. In this fourth box of mind consciousness everybody dies.

And now look in the fourth box and you'll find a fifth, and this is called animal consciousness; and inside it there's a sixth box called vegetable consciousness; and inside it still another, a seventh, called mineral consciousness. And these are the four lower kingdoms, the four boxes that are in the mind consciousness of the creature who lives in the fourth world, the fourth box.

In your Bible these four boxes are called the "valley of the shadow of death." And the word "shadow" is used because it conveys the idea that human life in the fourth box and human death in the fourth box are only shadows, shadows of your divine

Self. And it was Moses who presented these three upper kingdoms of your divine Self and the four lower kingdoms of your shadow self and called them the seven days of Genesis. That was his mystical code to explain the seven levels of consciousness through which every soul must travel. Divine life overflows into every level. And your soul journeying from divine life downward through the seven levels of consciousness must make the return upward back to its source.

We stand now in the fourth level, the fourth box, mind consciousness; and our soul is making its journey back to the three heavens above mind consciousness; and this is exactly the point where man stands at this moment.

We think we are looking at animals. We are not. We are looking at an animal consciousness through our mind consciousness, and that consciousness is made visible to us. We are not looking at human beings. We are looking at mind consciousness made visible, and as we rise to soul consciousness we will no longer see human beings because they only exist in our mind consciousness. Instead, we will see soul forms not made of human flesh and blood but made of light. **And right now, if you were in Soul consciousness, for you the human race would disappear.**

That is one reason why the Bible says, "God is no respecter of persons." God is not looking and seeing human form. Behind all this is a great secret and a great mystery. The four lower kingdoms in time have no reality. That is why they perish. The three upper kingdoms outside time are reality. That is why they are eternal.

The human race in the fourth box must always reach a bottleneck and become stagnant, isolated from its own divine self, imprisoned within the mind consciousness. And here it must turn from leader to leader, from promise to promise, desperately praying for miracles. But the horrors continue in this fourth box. The big nations continue to swallow the small nations. Today's ally becomes tomorrow's enemy. Governments collapse overnight. Blood flows on the streets and on the battlefields of the world.

There are heart attacks, open heart surgery, drugs, alcoholism, divorces, abortions, miscarriages, birth control pills, weight control pills, sleeping pills, pain pills, out-of-sight medical and hospitalization bills, runaway food prices, mass suicides, racism, fear, insecurity, children starving, complete populations living in slavery or fear of invasion, millions wallowing in poverty with nothing to look forward to––only the gentle mercy of death. All this we find in the fourth level, the fourth box, the fourth world called mind consciousness.

Perhaps the biggest tragedy of all is that four billion people are standing in that fourth box, right now, stranded. They have reached a dead end but don't know it. Science offers them no way out. Religion says you must suffer and die before you go to heaven. The psychologist, the psychiatrist, the sociologist stroke their beards; and they offer well meaning advice. But invariably they deal only with the disturbing symptoms, and they overlook the one basic cause of all the problems in the fourth box because they are unaware of the mystical code of the Bible.

With all the propaganda issued about the super intelligence of computers, you would think that by now we could all feed the world problems into one bank of computers, then take a coffee break while the computers automatically solve everything. But no computer has been able to do this, and the reason is that God did not create computers. That's why no computer devised by science can tell you anything about your soul consciousness, your spiritual consciousness and your divine consciousness. But you, even without a course in computer engineering and without seven years of premed and medical school, without psychoanalysis or anthropological research, you can quickly easily discover why the human race is stagnant and suffering and dying in the fourth box.

Suppose you try to answer one simple question. It's an important question, and I'd like you to answer it in two ways. The first way is the way a child of ten would answer it. And so I'd like you to go back to your tenth birthday. Try to recapture the mind level of a ten-year-old. Just see yourself as a ten-year-old boy or a ten-year-old girl, and then when you feel that to some degree you can imagine yourself back on your tenth birthday, prepare yourself now to answer this simple question: When did your life begin?

Remember now, you're ten years old and the question is: When did your life begin? Alright. Now let's jump ahead. Let's come back to your present age, and let's answer that question from your adult mind. And so here's the question again, but now the question is put to you as an adult: When did your life begin? Alright. Now we have two answers, and let's analyze both of them.

As a ten-year-old child your answer probably would have been, "My life began ten years ago." And now as an adult, a normal adult, your answer would have been that if your birthday is 42 years ago, that your life began 42 years ago. Right? Whatever your age you would normally say my life began that many years ago. Now maybe some of us are a little more advanced than that, but as you know, most of the world thinks that way. The majority of people believe that their lives began on their birthday. And most people would answer that their life began therefore either on the day when they were born or, if they wanted to be a little more technical, on the day that they were conceived in their mother's womb. Now can you see the error of that belief? Can you see the catastrophe of that belief? If not, you will in a moment.

Let's return to your mother and your father before you were born, while you were being carried by your mother; and let's see what they were thinking. Chances are they were wondering if the birth would be easy, whether you'd be a boy or a girl, what you'd look like, who you'd take after, if you'd be healthy and good-natured, how much you'd weigh and things of that nature. And if you had brothers and sisters and grandparents, everyone in the family would be waiting to welcome this new life that was being born into the family. Because as far as anyone was aware, your life was just beginning. Your parents were bringing a new life into this world. Now right there, please stop.

6

That was the consciousness under which you probably were born. And if so, you have just done what no computer can ever do. You have located the root, the epicenter, the nucleating core which causes all suffering and all death of the human race on this earth. You have gone past the symptoms direct to the center of man's unsolved problem.

The instant that we confuse human birthdays with the beginning of our lives, we surrender our divine heritage; and we separate ourselves from the life and protection of God. We've all done it. From that moment on, the great power and wisdom of divine life cannot sustain us. We become mortal branches that inevitably must wither and die. This is the innocent blunder committed by most parents in our world, perpetuated from generation to generation for centuries beyond count. And the shocking truth of that blunder becomes clear if you take a moment to consider a tree, and just watch the life flowing through the tree, through the trunk. Watch the life of that tree forming a branch, and out of the branch sprouts a twig. A branch, a twig, two different forms, but both produced by the same life. Now watch the life flow through the twig and form a leaf, a new form, but again the same life substance.

Always the one life substance becomes another form. Now it becomes a flower, then a fruit. Each form is actually a womb for the life substance to produce another form. And always, *always*, the life substance exists before the birth of the fruit, before the birth of the flower, before the birth of the twig, before the birth of the branch, before the birth of the trunk; and the same life substance exists before it becomes a tree. One life, many forms. And always that life preexists all the forms. So with mankind.

The life of your mother existed before she appeared in form. Her life did not begin in her mother's womb. Every ancestor in your family tree appeared the same way. The same indivisible life ran through your entire family tree. Always, each mother thought a new life was beginning in her womb. Each thought that her womb was the beginning of a new life which was different than the life before her, different than her life, different than her mother's life. But she was wrong. Just as one life did not begin in a branch or in a twig or in a leaf, but existed long before the leaves sprouted, that same life remained after the leaves died and produced new leaves. So with human beings. Your life did not begin in your mother's womb. It could not. And without this knowledge you cannot fulfill your life purpose.

The function of motherhood is different than most mothers suspect. The highest responsibility of an expectant mother is not taught by gynecologists, nor is it mentioned by Dr. Spock. It is the expectant mother's sacred responsibility to know consciously that divine life, divine spirit and divine soul are the reality of the form that is pressing through her into visibility. Every mother and every father are the child's only link to its own divine Self, its own divine life; and unless mother and father know this for the unborn child, that child will be born into mortal consciousness, mind consciousness, and will not know itself as divine life but will know itself as form. And by the age of two or three, that child will be committed to a life separated from the qualities of its own divinity.

Woman is the crossroad between divine life and mortal form, between immortality and mortality. She can be Eve, and she can bring forth mortal children who automatically are banished from Eden (Eden meaning divine life), or she can be Mary and bring forth an immortal child, who never leaves the Kingdom of God and is forever united with God in the grace and the glory of oneness.

Every father has the same opportunity. Every father can be Adam, believing in the material tree of life, the material tree of good and evil; or every father can be Joseph, awake to the knowledge that the divine life of God is the only life and that the only reality of the unborn child is that perfect divine life.

When parents are aware of the three heavens which constitute the divine life, spirit and soul of their child, this birth is a virgin birth. When parents are unaware, this birth is called the fall. And that's the true mystical meaning behind the biblical statement that man has fallen, not that he has sinned. He has fallen from the knowledge of his own divinity. And it is for this specific reason that Christ urges each of us to be reborn of the Spirit, to be as perfect as our divine Father. It is difficult to realize that your divine life and God's life are the same, but it is true. It is easier to realize that God's life did not begin in your mother's womb, and that, too, is true. God's life, which is your divine life, always existed. And because God's life is the only life, it is your life, your only life; and that means you have always existed.

When your parents, and you, accepted human birth as your beginning, millions of years of divine life were tossed away. And it is this divine life that each of us tossed away that holds the sacred answers for every need, every problem that we have been unable to solve. It is a truism, and a fortunate one for all of us, that death is absolutely unnecessary. Suffering is absolutely unnecessary. Nor is it necessary for any of us to keep stumbling in the darkness of mortality waiting for another savior to come to earth.

You and I have a choice. You may continue as you are. You may continue living in the fourth box of mind consciousness. You may continue trying to improve your human conditions, solving your human problems with human methods; or you can step out of your human rhythm into your divine rhythm, and you can open the fifth box. Opening the fifth box is how we enter the three heavens. And, of course, there is a divine plan to help you do this.

Just a few days ago these very words that you are listening to now on tape were not on tape. They were floating around in the ozone. They were waiting for a channel to express them, and there you were in your city and here I was in Kauai with an ocean between us. But now distance has lost its meaning, and these words are uniting us in oneness just the same as if we were both sitting in the same room. And even if you were to turn off your tape recorder right now, the words would still be there ready to be heard at any moment that you wish to hear them.

Now what about your other tape recorder? I mean the one within you. You have one, you know. It has a different voice on it, the voice of your own divine life. And it's been placed within you to lead you, to guide you out of the perishable into the imperishable, out of mind consciousness into soul consciousness, out of the fourth box called this world into the fifth box, the first heaven. And there you have, very graphically, the divine plan to lift you out of the wheel of birth and death into eternal life now. Your own infinite life force flowing down from the three topmost levels of consciousness invites you to lay hold of eternal life and to be lifted up, up, up, up the mystical ladder, out of the fourth box where everyone dies.

The secret of the mystics of all ages, and the precise purpose of your human life, is to surrender your mind consciousness to your Soul; and your soul consciousness will take you the rest of the way into paradise. Either you climb the ladder of mysticism beyond mind consciousness or, as you know, you perish in mind consciousness. That is divine law, but it is also divine wisdom.

"Seek ye first the Kingdom of God and his righteousness, and all things will be added unto you." Now that Kingdom is the three levels of your consciousness above your mind, and you don't have to wait for that Kingdom. It isn't going to return; it never went away. It's right here, because that Kingdom is you. Before your first human birthday that Kingdom was you, and it is you even now while your mind consciousness may be thinking of you as a physical form with a temporary life.

Let's be still a moment. Let's dwell in the truth that I am divine being now. And know yourself not as the world sees you, not as your friends see you, not as your children see you, not even as your parents see you. Know yourself as God sees God, as divine life without opposite. This is the real nature of illumination or enlightenment.

Illumination is not what most people think it is. It's not a flashing vision or even the voice of God coming to you maybe once every five or ten years. Illumination is awakening to the truth that you are not the form born in your mother's womb. You are the divine life of God that always was, that is now and always will be, and that you are not confined in the fourth box called mind consciousness. And when you dedicate your waking hours to accepting your divine life as a now fact, not a future event, your soul buds will really open up. They will receive heavenly manna from your divine life. And the entire contents of the three heavens will flow through you, through your Soul, into your mind;s and they will exchange your lifespan for your permanent life.

I'd like to repeat that idea in another way. Unless you accept divine life now as the truth of you and you strive to understand that human life is only a concept without substance, you will actually delay your attainment of soul consciousness and delay your rebirth.

Now how to develop soul consciousness is the subject of these seven mystical tapes. Before October rolls around for the seminar we hope to find out more about our own immortal life stream. We hope to release ourselves from the false belief that our lives began with human birth. We hope to discover that we can with total confidence place our trust in our own divine life to provide living substance for everything we need at every level of consciousness along the way. We're actually saying goodbye to the fourth box that counterfeits the Kingdom of God, and we're saying hello to our true life that can never know death. We're saying, "Speak Father, thy Son heareth."

We're joining hands and hearts in our one divine self, in our one divine life which flows invisibly as one life, the life of all. We are letting that divine life lead us into the realization of our own immortality now. And this is our preparation for the twenty-five lessons or twenty-six or -seven more that will follow in the seven mystical tapes.

LESSON 2: IMPORTANT MEDITATIONS

For your second lesson today I would like now to move into several important meditations. The first one is this: Your divine life is present and functioning. It is alive. It is doing something. It is expressing. Your divine life can only express when you have accepted it through your Soul. It cannot enter your mind directly. Now the meditation, then, is this; the subject is: **Divine law can only function In divine life.**

I want you to reach above the mind to understand this truth, that divine life can only enter you as you accept the presence of your Soul. In the absence of your Soul you have no faculty with which to receive divine life. So now carefully isolate this one thought and do it throughout tomorrow in thirty seconds: **I am conscious that my Soul is present. I am conscious that my Soul is present.** Then rest in the silence for thirty seconds knowing your Soul is present.

If it bursts into flame as it were within you, stay with it. If you feel something digging roots within you, stay with it. But be sure at other times when you don't stay with it that you at least give it thirty seconds of inner recognition during the day. **Give it thirty seconds of recognition during the day and do it thirty different times a day for the first day.**

You will see what I mean. You will become conscious that you have been neglecting your own Soul by not even being aware of its presence, just lightly assuming that it's around somewhere. But now let's go deeper. It's not only present, it is the link between all you had thought you were on this earth and your divine life. How can your divine life function without your Soul as the intermediary? Your Soul now is bigger than your human body. Your Soul is bigger than your human brain. Your Soul is bigger than your human mind. Your Soul never thinks human thoughts. Your thought is the channel for divine thought. **But you are your Soul. Your Soul is you**. Let's get out of this little you, who is doing the meditation, into the knowledge that **I am my Soul.**

My Soul is not only present, it is I. I am my Soul now. My Soul isn't confined anywhere. My Soul fills this entire room. Therefore I, I fill this entire room. My Soul goes much farther than that, but I'll stay with this for a moment. My Soul, which I am, fills this room. What else is here? My Spirit and my Life. What else is here? Nothing else.

Your Spirit, your Life, your Soul are all there is of you. They are infinite. They are three in one. Your divine Self flows through your Spirit and through your Soul. Your Spirit flows through your divine Self and through your Soul. Your Soul flows through your Spirit and your divine Life. Three in one, all you.

My divine Life is here now, flowing through my Spirit here now, through my Soul here now. I can rest. And my divine Life flowing through my Soul will express all that God is.

It is very vital that you establish without any duality an appreciation of the present nature of your living Soul, your living Spirit, your living divine Life, for they are all independent of this world of form.

Thirty times tomorrow: ***My Soul Is Present. I Am My Soul. My Soul Fills All Space And Beyond. I Fill All Space And Beyond.***

Eventually you will become conscious of yourself outside physical form, outside a physical world, outside physical powers. You will feel a new freedom, a new self. Now resting in this we move on to other ideas of our infinite being. My Soul consciousness reveals:

I am not flesh and blood. I am not dying matter. I am that life substance which has no blemish. I am pure immortal life. I am the immaculate expression of God being. I need struggle for nothing. My God substance is all I am, and it contains all I need. My substance can never manifest less than the pure eternal perfection of God. I am that substance. I am the living Soul that receives that substance. I am not a world mind picture. I am not a body. I am not an image without substance. I am not a shadow of thought.

∞∞∞∞∞∞∞∞∞∞ End of Side One ∞∞∞∞∞∞∞∞∞∞

But be assured that your divine life has a perfect divine plan and perfect divine wisdom to teach you how to live divinely, and to teach you how to communicate this truth to others as they become ready for it. But remember, before you think of teaching others, you have a sacred responsibility to leave your nets and to learn for yourself how to move into the fifth world, how to connect your mind with your Soul, to apply it, to prove it on your own life before you try communicating it to anyone else.

There is something very beautiful about truth. When you get a little of it, it seems to expand; and that's what's happening right now. Truth is expanding within us. And it is when this happens that you recognize it is truth, because truth is never stagnant. It is always growing.

LESSON 3: HUMAN BIRTH

Now let's return to the days just before your human birth. Refresh your mind with what was in your mother's mind at that time, and as you think about it, you can be certain of one thing. She was not thinking about herself as divine life, divine spirit, divine soul. Nor was she thinking that the child forming inside her was the infinite divine life that stretches way back for millions of years before the world began. It's more reasonable, as we originally presumed, that her thoughts were about you, your health, whether you'd be well formed, what color your eyes might be, would you be big or small, how long would she labor, things of that nature.

Now right here is the giant step, and it is a question that you have never been asked by anyone since the very first day that you appeared on earth. Carefully think of the precise moment just before your mother gave birth to you and ask yourself, "Where were you at that moment? Where were you just before your body was born?" Well, I did say it was a strange question.

Now you know and I know that out of five million people probably five million will automatically respond, "Well, I was in my mother's womb waiting to enter this world." Were you? Is that where you were? Are you sure that's where you were? Have you been studying that you are divine life? That you are eternal spirit? That you are the immortal soul? That you are the one indivisible life that has always existed? That you are the divine life of God? That you are the divine life that can never be sick or die? Is that the life that was in your mother's womb? Are you beginning to see where we're heading?

You are about to discover a strange phenomenon. One that has escaped the attention of the entire medical profession, all of science and practically all of the religious leaders in our world. Who is this child in your mother's womb just a few moments before an infant body emerged? Was it you? Is a material body divine? How do we even know that that body will make it into this world?

There are many mothers who decide to have these embryos aborted. Would these mothers have power to abort a divine child? Could there be a stillborn divine child or the miscarriage of a divine child? And yet there are hundreds of thousands of miscarriages and stillborn babies every year. Thousands are born deformed or retarded. How could a divine child be born deformed or retarded? How could a divine child ever become sick, diseased, disabled? How could a divine child become evil, corrupt, deceitful, starving, debilitated or stricken by a virus or a heart attack? Could a divine child become a terminal case of leukemia or have a heart disease or end up in a sanitarium waiting for the final curtain fall? Do you see? A divine child couldn't even die. All these things cannot happen to divine life, but they happen to millions of children who emerge from the womb of woman.

Now please, we are into mysticism, so listen very closely to the most unusual truth that you may ever have heard. That child in your mother's womb could not have been you. You were never in your mother's womb. That was the message of Jesus when he said to his mother, "Woman, what have I to do with you? I am the life." And you too, and your mother too, and your father too, and your grandparents; all must realize you were never in a material womb. And it's difficult isn't it, but it's the truth you must know to know God aright. For God is all, God life is all, and God's life never entered your mother's womb.

When you become really conscious of yourself as divine life, not physical life, you will then understand how impossible it is for eternal infinite divine life to divide itself into fractions and to enter the temporary womb of a woman. You will see that your divine life has no human opposite and that the illusion of Spirit entering matter has deceived the mind consciousness of mankind.

Something did happen, of course, on your so-called human birthday. You may, if you wish, think of it as a shadow of your Soul. For as your Soul passes from one level of consciousness to the next, something happens which we interpret as becoming a mineral, a vegetable, an animal or a human being. But one thing is certain––your human birth was not the birth of your permanent self. It couldn't be, because your permanent self already existed. Your divine life has no birthday, no death day, no suffering day. Your divine life will never be shattered by a hydrogen or neutron bomb.

On your birthday a new mind consciousness was born, and it was born in the world mind; and it was a consciousness separated from God, separated from divine life, from spirit and soul. It was a consciousness limited to the five primitive senses of touch, hearing, smelling, tasting, seeing. It knew nothing outside of itself, nothing outside of its mentality, nothing outside of its mentally conceived form; and even when it matured, it had no way of knowing that it was only a shadow of its own reality. It was just a tiny mental cell in a vast body, thinking of itself as a separate and individual body. Everything about it was reduced to a small counterfeit scale model.

It reduced one infinite life to an interval called a lifespan, and the infinite newness of life appeared as a form breathing in-out, in-out. The infinite circulation of grace throughout your immortal spiritual body appeared as the circulating bloodstream of the human body. Eternity became time. Infinity became space. Unlimited dimensions would dwarf down to three dimensions. Everything real was fragmented, finitized and converted mentally. And in the center of this miniature re-creation lived a tiny cell of consciousness hypnotized into the belief that it was a man or a woman, aware of nothing outside the fourth box which we know as the fourth world, and completely unaware that the temporary nature of its lifespan was because all of it from birth to death—— even its so-called human identity——was made of sense impressions picked out of cosmic energy from invisible waves that are called electromagnetic by the scientist, by five feeble antennae that we call five senses. All this recorded, converted, projected by your brain into a mental image which walks the earth called form.

Every human mind consciousness is a prisoner of cosmic energy. Humans are actually little relay systems for this ultra-speed invisible energy. They feed on it. They transform fractions of it into picture images that they call form, world, people, things, objects. And as we grow higher in our capacity to develop receptivity to this cosmic energy, great inventions and discoveries pour forth; and our hopes soar. We envision vast breakthroughs into unexplored mysteries. But inevitably, whenever a mind consciousness crumbles, the action of the body crumbles with it. We must be very alert, very perceptive; and if we are and we look very closely, we discover that divine life and the cosmic energy that activates the human lifespan and the human body are not one and the same.

The scientist is right when he says he cannot see God in the human scene. God is not with mortals; we know that. And when the scientist talks about human evolution, he's really talking about the evolution of cosmic energy in this fourth world. Inside the body formed by your mind consciousness you are controlled and limited, and you are forced to live a temporary false lifespan, which as you know by now is not governed by God, but is governed by the false power of cosmic energy which animates you until it finally kills you. And God does absolutely nothing about it.

But when you learn to shift out of human evolution into your soul consciousness, instead of being human clay molded by cosmic mind, your Soul takes over. You become the sculptor instead of the clay. Then your evolution is no longer inside cosmic energy which dies, but in soul energy which lives forever. You're then a spiritual traveler. You're released from false identity. You're reborn to your own divine life.

We must face this, because until you are ready to accept––1. You were not born in the womb of woman––2. You never were in the womb of woman–– you are not accepting divine life. And as long as divine life is not what you accept is your true identity, you are really divided from your Self. Denying your flesh on one hand is not enough. Accepting your Spirit on the other hand is not enough. You must do both. To accept your Spirit you must deny your flesh, and when you deny your flesh you must accept your Spirit. Then you will be rid of the conflict of seeking God, seeking the treasures of the Kingdom while you are still laboring under the conflict of both the flesh and the Spirit.

This so-called conflict between flesh and Spirit is actually the division between your Soul and your mind. When you prepare to unite Soul and mind, you are on the way to repairing the breach. And as you mend this breach as Soul surrenders to Spirit and Spirit surrenders to divine Life, so mind must surrender to Soul to provide the continuity from the highest to the fourth realm; and then you will escalate out of duality into oneness, out of dying lifespans into life. And then you will discover you are prepared to face all appearances in this world with the tested knowledge that the only you, the real you, is not physical form imprisoned in the fourth box.

We're very grateful to all the mystics who wrote the Bible and all the other great scriptures. It was difficult for them to communicate divine truth to the masses, as you know, but they had an inner integrity which forced them to preserve their truth in a mystical code.

Paul, as you know, realized that everything in the fourth box was a fiction, a picture image. He had touched the third heaven, had realized his divine life, had experienced his own immortality while on earth; and he recognized that Moses had also experienced the deathless self while he walked the earth. If you recall the astounding seventh chapter of Paul's epistle to the Hebrews, you can see clearly that Paul was explaining a very great secret taught by Moses and bringing this secret to the attention of his, Paul's, disciples. That's why he wrote, "Melchizedek is without father, without mother, without descent, having neither beginning of days nor end of life, but made like unto the Son of God."

What was Paul saying? He was teaching that Melchizedek had realized himself to be eternal divine life, not human flesh, not cosmic energy, not a human being who must die. But now comes another great truth. "Consider," says Paul, "how great Melchizedek was, unto whom even the patriarch Abraham gave a tenth of the spoils."

That's high mysticism. Abraham tithing to Melchizedek means that Abraham also recognized his own divine life. That's the mystical code that he, too, was without father, without mother, without descent, without beginning or end, but that he was the eternal Son of God. And this, mind you, was before Jesus Christ. Divine life recognized is Christ consciousness, and it is the secret of every true prophet whoever walked this earth. It's the song of Solomon. It's the song of freedom sung by the mystics of all ages. But more important, it's the truth of you right now.

You know, every time there's a virgin birth there has to be a virgin death. You see this when Jesus is born without a physical contact between Mary and Joseph. That's really more than just an historical event. It's a mystical statement. It's a statement that the life of Jesus existed before his form emerged from the womb of Mary. Religion has not understood that divine life can never die, and there is no other. And, therefore, crucifixion could not kill the virgin-born Jesus. The same divine life that existed before virgin birth continued to exist after the appearance of death, and that's a virgin death. Whoever accepts divine life is assured of a virgin death. And that is the hidden meaning of resurrection. Just as divine life is never born in the womb of woman, it never dies. But it is always present even while mind consciousness uses cosmic energy to create the illusion of birth and death in form.

Quietly now, it's necessary for you to dwell upon the truth that you never were in the womb of woman. And if you have believed that you reincarnated fifty times, then you should know that in those fifty so-called mothers that you had, you never were in one of the fifty wombs. You are divine life which never enters the material womb, and that is the purpose of your meditation: To realize the truth of it first intellectually, and then to let the Spirit and the Soul flow into your consciousness to reveal to you the truth of eternal divinity in a way you never really suspected.

[pause]

We will go directly into our fourth lesson.

LESSON 4: WOMB OF LIFE

No mother can ever give birth to divine life. No man and woman through physical contact can ever create divine life. It already exists. It is the God-given reality of every man, woman and child. Unfortunately, this wonderful truth has been buried for centuries while mankind has been forced to slush through the mud of original sin, divine punishment and fictitious rewards in a heavenly hereafter. One hundred million mothers who give birth every year have been told to put on the garment of immortality, but they did not understand. Instead, they have been denying the divine life of the infant consciousness that they have born into the world. When one of them stops and restores the divine heritage to one of these unborn children, that child will grow up aware of its divine life. When one mother blesses a child with its true identity and protects it with the consciousness of its own identity, and knows her identity as divine life, and knows that the true father of that child is divine life, and that the true identity of herself and the child is the same one divine life, that child will be made free.

Oh yes, I'm sure it would shock those one hundred million mothers to learn that if they fail to identify their newborn children as divine life and falsely identify them as flesh, those children will not be under the law of God; and they will be forced to spend the next fifty or sixty years wondering why the children they have born have grown into adulthood and still walk without divine protection.

All of the human prayer in the world is not going to change a human being to divine grace, to divine power, to divine substance. It must be done by the expectant mother, by the expectant father, in order to give the child a beginning in truth. And when it is not done, then it becomes necessary for the child to learn it as he or she grows up.

When Paul declared, "This mortal must put on immortality," he was stating a divine law, a law that cannot be violated. Your change of consciousness from mortal to immortal, from form life to divine life, is not something you can take lightly. It is not optional. Rebirth was taught by Jesus as more than a pledge that you make with your lips, more than a change of morals. Rebirth taught by Jesus is reunion with your eternal divine life, which never was born in your mother's womb.

Please remember this: "Every child born on earth is outside the law of God because God is no respecter of persons." And no human opinion will change that. And that child remains outside the law of God until the mother or that child itself learns to put on the garment of immortality. The consciousness of its own

21

immortal divine life here, now, today; not one hundred or two hundred years later when a savior returns to earth.

Now there are many corruptions of this sacred truth. One of them is the belief that your material body will someday become spiritual. And another corruption is the belief that your material body already is spiritual. Neither are true. Probably behind both of these false beliefs is the desire to remain in a body of flesh, trying to be both mortal and immortal at the same time. But, says the Master, "No man can serve two masters; ye cannot serve God and mammon."

In other words, you cannot live in divine life and in human life at the same time. And if you're not living in divine life, you're living in mammon. The consequences are these: ***Divine life must live forever. Mammon must die.*** It's quite that simple.

And so Jesus was really saying, "Choose life. Don't choose death." And now it's necessary for us to catch the distinction that the human sense of life, which lives in the body of dying flesh—oh, this is so important to catch! That human sense of life that lives in a body of dying flesh is not you, and this human sense of life which dies has never been you. That all human flesh is a cosmic concept. That all life within human flesh is an animated shadow in the mind. And this is the mystical understanding of the word "mammon" taught by Jesus in the sixth chapter of Matthew, verse 24. Divine life cannot flow in mortal flesh. Divine life cannot flow through the material womb of a mother who accepts mortal flesh and mortal life as her identity.

We really have no choice. If we continue to identify as mammon, not divine life, we cannot inherit the Kingdom of God. Whether it's spoken by Peter, Paul, Jesus or John, the mystical truth is always the same. God is not the creator of mortal flesh. God is no respecter of mortal flesh.

On the other hand, Jesus tells us, "Take no thought for your life." Why? Because the life that you worry about is not your life. The life that begins in your mother's womb and ends when your brain and your heart stop functioning is not your life. It's mental energy. Your real life, your divine life, is not influenced one bit by the birth or death of your physical form or the condition of your physical form, because divine life is never influenced by the mental shadow for which mankind has been taking thought through all these centuries.

Paul reminds us there is a natural body and there is a spiritual body. "The first man is of the earth, earthy; the second man is the Lord from heaven." Again, mystically speaking, Paul was revealing that salvation is not waiting for your reward in heaven, but now, here, accepting your divine life which he called the Lord from heaven, and then rising above the belief that your life lives inside an earthy form that must die.

Time and time again Paul keeps opening this doorway to truth for all men. "Awake thou that sleepest and Christ," meaning your true divine life, "will give thee light." Stop lingering in bodies of mental energy that you know must eventually die. It's that simple again. Stop claiming a life that began on a birthday and ends on a death day. Choose God life, not mammon life.

"As we are born the image of the earthy, we shall also bear the image of the heavenly." When Paul said that he was again telling mankind how to step out of the fourth box of a dying mind. "As we are born the image of the earthy, we shall also bear the image of the heavenly" by stepping out of the dying mind, the mind consciousness, the fourth box, into the fifth box, into our own eternal Soul.

Paul was so excited when he said this, because he knew he had an amazing discovery, that he couldn't resist adding a few words. "Behold, I show you a mystery. We shall not all sleep..." meaning, there are some among us who are able to understand what I am talking about, that the true miracle of life without beginning or end is the fact those who will grasp the real life which is forever. And then he adds,

"And they shall be changed, they shall all be changed in a moment, in the twinkling of an eye, for the trumpet shall sound and the dead shall be raised incorruptible, and we shall be changed. For the corruptible must put on incorruption, and this mortal must put on immortality."

What is that trumpet? That trumpet is your realization that you are divine life now. Who are the dead? The dead is a sleeping being and the sleeping human race trying to live in dying bodies. The corruptible is the temporary mortal body of flesh that eventually disintegrates. The incorruptible is your permanent immortal body of pure soul energy that never ages, never decays, never dies; your spiritual body which is activated by divine life, under divine law, always expressing the harmony of God. This awakened consciousness knows that it is immortal. This awakened consciousness never dies. This awakened consciousness knows that death has no existence.

It is the religious consciousness, still sleeping back there in the Middle Ages, that keeps singing the praises of Paul but does not share his wisdom. As a result, mankind today is continuing to sleep and to bear the miseries of his mortal dream. They're not accepting divine life in Afghanistan or in Iran, just as they didn't in Guyana. In our world today all countries are ignoring divine life while our physicians patch our bodies, while diseases ravage our bodies, while disasters destroy our bodies, old age cripples our bodies, bombs threaten our bodies;m and eventually all who have not heard the trumpet of divinity are forced to lay down their bodies, because unless we rise from the false deadness of mortal life we remain in the fourth box.

You know, during the past sixteen years every person who has come to me with a problem thought that he or she was seeking the solution to that particular problem. What they really were seeking was their own divine life. The problems were symptoms, evidence that they had not yet accepted divine life here and now. One problem could be a backache, another finances, a third would have a rocky marriage or a threat of malignancy, but the real solution always has been this––not how do I get rid of this problem––that's not the real solution. The real solution is: *How can I move out of mind consciousness into Soul consciousness that knows itself as divine life?*

That's the real solution. That's the mystical meaning of "Seek ye first the Kingdom." That's really the essential teaching of all the mystics and all the spiritual leaders. It's the secret of all the Hebrew prophets. Isn't that the understanding of Jesus Christ, Paul, Peter and John? Isn't that the underlying theme of the New and the Old Testaments? Isn't the Kingdom of God within you a revelation that you are divine life now? Isn't it that simple? Isn't every word in demonstration of Jesus Christ brought to an electrifying climax when he declares why he could accomplish these great things on earth? "I am the life," and it was that life accepted which performed every miracle and revealed every word that he spoke.

Our nets and the nets of mankind cannot be cast on the wrong side of the ship any longer. The human race seeks material improvements for material lives, and the results of that method are written in all the obituary columns on every newspaper. The key to survival, the key to salvation, is not bigger armies and navies and air forces; not hiding in an atom bomb shelter; not escaping on a satellite bound for Mars. The key to salvation and survival is living here and now in your own indestructible divine self. Instead of casting your nets in a sea of mortality, cast your nets into the divine ocean where there are no human lifespans that end, only one infinite eternal life without division; and your nets will bring forth the blessings of divine peace, divine love and harmony, divine supply, and every treasure of the divine Kingdom.

Remember you cannot fish in the divine ocean with your mortal mind. Only your Soul can fish on the spiritual immortal side of the ship. That's our direction, our opportunity and our dedication.

Between now and your next tape, please pick up a copy of *The Infinite Way* by Joel Goldsmith and read the fourth chapter, "Your Real Existence." When I say read it, I mean devour it. Know it better than you know your own name. You've got a whole month for that. Go over each paragraph; study it; analyze it. Try to see that he is giving you condensed wisdom and that every word is worth a thousand pictures instead of the other way around. He can say in one brief instant enough to fill ten more volumes. And so very carefully scrutinize those words and understand that they are speaking to you pure Christ truth.

Now also during the next month, please go over the four lessons here on this tape. You'll find quite a number of meditations, particularly in the second lesson. There is one in the first at the end of it, and there is one in the third. Pick them all up and do them two ways during the month. One, about yourself. But the second way is about your children or some others who are close to you, such as grandchildren. So that when you do a meditation on your own soul being present, the next time around do it to know that the soul of the child or grandchild is present. The divine life of grandchild or child is present, and in that way your meditations will begin to bear more fruit.

TAPE 2

LESSONS 5 - 7

Herb: Greetings from the island of Kauai.

It seems that just yesterday many of us were here on the island sharing the Easter seminar. There have been many events since then, many experiences, many progressions, perhaps many painful lessons. But there has been something that may truthfully be called progress.

LESSON 5: BEING CONSCIOUS OF THE PRESENCE

We have entered into a higher level of consciousness. Many of us now have a broader base of confidence in what we're doing, who God is, how God functions in our lives. And, of course, there are some who still are reaching out for that magic button which they hope will bring everything into focus.

What we are learning is that the life of divine Spirit does not exist inside a human form. We're learning why the Bible tells us that God is no respecter of persons. We're learning about the mystical code of the ancients telling us how to get out of the body of flesh before we die. And, of course, rebirth is not a simple process. It's very painful to those who resist it, and even when we try to cooperate with the divine instruction we receive, there is inevitably a feeling that may be called strangeness because your consciousness is adjusting to a new rhythm. It's somewhat like the itching of a scab. It bothers you, but you're happy about it too because it's a sign that your wound is almost healed.

It was probably strange to you during your spiritual lifespan to realize that you were never in your mother's womb. Maybe you're still fighting with that idea. But I tell you it's even stranger to discover that the Easter resurrection of Jesus Christ has been telling you just that for the past twenty centuries. That's what the resurrection of Jesus is all about. The proof that there is a life that exists which never was born in the womb of woman and never began in the womb of woman and never was even in the womb of woman. And because we have missed that through the years, we have missed the meaning of the Easter resurrection.

Since the last tape there have been some interesting reports to me about a strange and wonderful kind of progress. And I think what it really is, is that you have uprooted old concepts that you didn't even know you had. And in so doing you have to some degree reunited yourself with the will of God. You're going to become more and more of a channel for that divine will. You're going to increase your receptivity to it by being aware of its presence and by being obedient to it. And you will notice that not only does your life stabilize, but it will develop an aura of enchantment, a sort of sense of freedom that is quite unearthly.

Today on these three or four tapes, whatever it turns out to be, I mean three or four lessons, we want to open ourselves to divine will. We want you to know that divine will is where you are in your room right now. Let's catch that. We've all been talking about the presence of God, practicing the presence of God, practicing the omnipresence of God. Right in your room right now is God, and where God is, the will of God is.

Two hours from now in human time, if you are consciously aware of the presence of the will of God where you are, you will have discovered more than most of mankind has discovered during the past twenty centuries of the presence of the will of God is the beginning of your daily divine communication, the beginning of your divine rhythm, the end of your world karma and your individual karma. Because all these are––this world and individual karma––is the failure of man to find the will of God, the communication of God, and the divine living. And man has failed to do this for a simple reason: Not knowing the will of God, he spends every day violating that will.

All around you world upheavals––recessions, talk about depression, war, catastrophe, fear, discord, insecurity, every disturbance you know––and all those little unexpected crises that creep into our lives unwanted, unforeseen, these happen because human flesh is separated from the will of God. And without contact with the wisdom and the power of divine will, the human race is tossed blindly on a sea of uncontrolled conditions. But the moment that man reunites with divine will something happens that is truly miraculous. Storms become gentle; pain becomes less painful; blood stops flowing. The impossible dream becomes a shining reality.

We have been living most of our human lives by our own human will, and every moment that we fulfill our human will, we violate divine will. There is simply no way that we can fulfill human will and divine will at the same time except by letting divine will be our only will. I don't think we have to enumerate the results of this tragic error. It has already been written on the battlefields and the tombstones that are scattered all over the world. Human will leads to the grave. That's a simple fact we cannot deny. Divine will leads to eternal life.

Human will ignores divine will in every possible way or it denies it, challenges it, rejects it, adulterates it, pretends it doesn't even exist. Sometimes it reluctantly obeys divine will, that is, whenever convenient. But the incredible fact is that violating divine will is the normal, natural, daily way of life for mankind.

All the great men of science do it. The Congress of the United States does it. Our educational system does it. Big business does it. Leaders of nations do it. Every religion on earth does it. They talk about God, pray to God, tithe to God, teach our children to worship God. But day in, day out the human will of man violates the divine will of God. In fact, it's so commonplace to do this that it's truly a universal violation. And no one recognizes it, so the world continues violating divine will; and the suffering that inevitably results continues to plague the human race.

In the Easter seminar there was one pitfall, one danger zone which we generally fall into, and it was said that...it was said at the time, "Do not make your own rules." Remember that? "Do not skip those Bible passages that you don't understand. Don't skip those spiritual principles that you find difficult or inconvenient."

Well, that wasn't just leveled at you. That's what mankind has done. The human race has actually been running away from the will of God, keeping its right hand on the Bible and violating God's will with its left hand. It would surprise half the world, I think, to discover that God really has a will, a living will; and that the will of God is always present.

Millions think that they are discharging their full obligation to God by trying to obey the Ten Commandments. Other millions believe that church membership entitles them to check in with God on Sunday and to spend the rest of the week pursuing their own human wills. And there are others brainwashed into the belief that as long as they live clean, honest, respectable lives; cheating nobody; fulfilling their human responsibilities and serving their communities that they have earned salvation. The tragedy of all this is that billions of sincere dedicated worshipers who genuinely want to obey the will of God do not know what the will of God is or where it is or how to obey it, and so they never stop violating the will of the God that they are trying to worship.

It's certainly not divine will that we have cancer on earth, but yet millions of people who think they are obeying God's will have cancer. It's not God's will that boys die on battlefields, but millions of parents who thought they were obeying God's will have had to send their boys to war. And it certainly was not God's will that millions of these boys never came home. Something went wrong. We've got to find out what it was. It's not God's will that old age reduces millions of people to weak shriveling shadows of their former selves, but it happens everyday. We've got to find out why.

What's the real problem? Why do these people continue to be victimized? And underneath it all you'll discover good people, bad people, rich people, poor people, all kinds of people including the most wonderful people in the world have never made contact with the will of God. They sought it. Perhaps they settled for some traditional form of worship. Perhaps they were tranquilized into the belief that they would receive divine blessings by leading the good life. They may have been like the Pharisees, fulfilling every jot and tittle of the religious law with absolute fidelity, but (inaudible) ever told them that sincerity, goodness and dedication are not enough. Shocking? Yes, but being a good human being is not enough.

You can fulfill the letter of every religious law on earth. You can fulfill the Ten Commandments, and you can still violate the will of God because divine will does not function through religion or through human flesh. **Divine will functions only through your Soul.** Divine will is no respecter of religions, no respecter of persons, no respecter of honesty or goodness, no respecter of human deeds. **Divine will functions only through your Soul.**

You see, we have made our own rules. We say, "Oh I'm very righteous. I'm loving. I'm law-abiding. I'm a faithful husband, a faithful wife. I'm a loyal employee. I'm a considerate employer. I'm a friend to my fellow man. I'm a pillar of my society." Yes, these are all commendable traits, but divine will demands more than that. Divine will demands more than human righteousness, more than loyalty, more than human love, more than every form of human goodness, or else you will continue to violate divine will. And because of your violation, you will not find the divine rhythm that leads to the Easter resurrection. You see, God makes the rules, not human beings. Whenever we substitute we separate ourselves from the will of God.

Now let's see how we can rectify our human error. You know and I know that most of us say at time to time, "I've looked everywhere for the will of God. I've sat here very patiently, cleared my mind. I've waited, I've waited, I've waited. Where is the will of God? I'm willing. God doesn't seem to be recognizing that I'm here looking, waiting, seeking, yearning for that will. Doesn't come." Oh, I tell you when I hear that I feel sad because I know the will is right there where that individual's heart is yearning to receive the will, and the blockage is very strange.

If you will examine your own experience, you'll discover that God presents His will to you in two ways. The first one must be obeyed before the second way will work. The first way is by divine messenger, such as the Old Testament prophets and Jesus Christ, Paul, Peter and so forth. These divine messengers prepare you for the second phase, and when you have obeyed phase one, phase two begins, not before usually. In phase two, instead of receiving the will of God from his divine messengers, you receive the will of God directly through your Soul. But unless you have been obedient to the divine will expressed through the divine messengers, your mind remains closed, unable to receive that which you seek.

It is in our obedience to the Spirit of scripture that the doors of our minds are unlocked. Cobwebs of concept are dissolved. The darkness is overshadowed by the light, and then you are led across the threshold of all mental limitation into the realm of Soul perception. And here through Soul communication, direct communication with divine will, you are lifted out of the valley of the shadow of death, out of a body that ages and dies, out of the imitation selfhood that has never been the perfect image and likeness of God.

Do you feel the presence of God in your room? Then also feel the presence of God's will. Feel it all around you. Feel it in the midst of you. It can never leave you. It is always there. Remember, this will of God planted in the midst of you is the greatest friend you will ever have. You may not know the way, but it knows the way to paradise. You can trust it. Be true to it, worship it, serve it without question, serve it without fear; and the world around you will be transformed. The will of God in the midst of you will take you, lift you, lead you, guide you, love you, protect you. It will lead you through the jaws of death untouched. It will place the purple robe of the immortal Son around you.

The secret of opening your Soul is to surrender to the divine will within you, to die daily to your human will. For in the degree that you die to human will, in like measure you will be reborn to divine will. Keep feeling the presence of divine will. This is a twenty-four-hour-a-day reality.

"I am never far off," says the will of God. *"I am where you are. I am here now, waiting for you to accept Me. Come unto Me. Surrender your human will to Me. Acknowledge Me. Trust Me. Fear not, for I lay down My life for My children."*

This has always been your choice. Unfortunately, the prodigal mind of man has been too busy with its own will to notice that the will of God is always present, always powerful, always wise, always all-knowing, always offering God Life, eternal life, perfect life; and the secret is that you must be willing to worship at your Soul level, not your mind level.

"Be my Son," says the will of God. *"Let me be your divine counselor. Let me be your will. Let our will be one will, and you will walk this earth here and now under Grace as the living Son of the living God."*

There have been some who obeyed this, but not those who walk this earth today. If you look across the globe at the homeless, the destitute, the disillusioned, the helpless and the hopeless millions, the broken families, the broken careers, the broken lives, the wasted lives haphazardly wandering without direction; if you look at your own struggles, and if you look at youth struggling, seeking guidance, seeking stability; if you look at the anguish and despair, the senseless waste of human lives mangled by wars, diseases, depressions, poverty; if you look at the millions of senior citizens tossed on the scrap heap just like worn out used cars, you've got to see the one thing missing in their lives was that they were without divine guidance because they had not found the present living will of God in their midst.

Why does man bloom like a flower, then wither, then scatter in the wind like lifeless dust? Is there anything under the sun that can help them——something that can deliver them from fear; from threats; from every form of jeopardy; from every type of suffering; from destruction; from evil; from failure, crime, disease, disaster, frustration, error; from every weakness? Why, of course, there is.

The miracle worker, the savior that every man seeks, the Messiah long awaited by the Hebrews is the will of God right in your room right now unseen by human eyes, unfelt by the human mind. The Redeemer of mankind, and our only Redeemer, is divine will planted in the midst of us before the world was and planted in our Bible by messengers to teach us how to break the separation between man's mind and man's Soul.

Do you feel that you are on the verge of seeing the nature of all human error? Can you feel the separation between your mind and your own soul? The will of God is in your soul now. You must learn how to let it reach your awareness. That's the purpose of scripture.

How many Hebrews understood Job when he said, "Man that is born of woman is of few days and full of trouble. He cometh forth like a flower and is cut down. He fleeth also as a shadow and continueth not."? Did we recognize those words as the will of God revealing through Job that the real man of Spirit is not the physical child born in a mother's womb?

How many Hebrews understood why Isaiah declared, "All flesh is grass."? Wasn't that the will of God telling us that the divine self of man is in a spiritual form that does not wither like grass. Did you notice that Peter was well aware of the meaning of Job's statement and of Isaiah's statement? And so Peter reminded us that the will of God always is expressing through the prophets. He wanted us to know that they weren't just talking to prophesy, that the will of God in them was expressing, and we were to follow that will.

"Prophecy," he said, "came not in old time by the will of man, but holy men of God spake as they were moved by the Holy Ghost." And how many Christians understood why Peter then quoted the prophecy of Isaiah, which mankind had heard but had not obeyed. How many Christians understood that Peter's statement was expressing the will of God for you and for me and for mankind; for every color skin; for men who walk under every flag of every nation; for the Greek, the Jew, the bond, the free, the male, the female.

Listen to the one great mystical truth behind Christianity, behind Judaism, Sufism, Taoism, Hinduism, Buddhism, every pure religion on earth. In the first epistle of Peter, chapter 1, verse 23, clearly expressed by Peter is God's purpose, God's will for you. "Being born again, not of corruptible seed, but of incorruptible, by the word of God, which liveth and abideth forever."

In other words: **Be reborn now into your permanent Self** because "...all flesh is as grass, and all the glory of man as the flower of grass. The grass withereth, and the flower thereof falleth away: But the word...,"––That is the divine life of God in every man, that's the word––"... the word of the Lord endureth for ever. And this is the Word which by the gospel is preached unto you." There it is––God's will that you get out of your body of grass that withers.

Peter was no scientist. He probably didn't know which came first, the atom or the molecule. But he knew something so astounding that no scientist seems to know. Science believes that the life of man begins with the union of the female ovum and the male sperm. God knows better. Moses knew better. Isaiah,

35

Samuel, Ezra, Daniel, Ezekiel, Solomon, Jeremiah, Habakkuk, Malachi, Peter, John—they all knew better.

Ah, but Jesus Christ not only knew better; he was more than a divine messenger. He was the living message itself. His very presence on earth was not created by the physical union of man and woman, but by the divine will of God revealing, demonstrating to man the presence of a life that is not a human life. The presence of a life that is independent of human form. The presence of a life that is not created by physical union between man and woman. The presence of a divine life that is neither made by flesh and blood nor enters into flesh and blood, a divine life that is not made of grass that withers, that is not like a flower that blooms and fades, but a divine life present on this earth, and I might add, in your room right now.

A life that never ages, never lacks, never fails, never dies. He was demonstrating a divine life that belongs to every man; a life that can never have a crooked arm, a blind eye, a malignant germ or a heart attack. And that divine life appearing on earth as Christ Jesus performing the miracles of restoration beyond all human power, that life was the living will of God saying to every man, "This is your divine life now. Walk ye in it."

Then in words of deathless fire, as if blazoned across the sky, the will of God declared, "He that hateth his life in this world shall keep it unto life eternal." [repeats] Modern religion teaches that man can be born again by giving up sin, doing good human deeds, and by saying, "I love you, Jesus. I love the Holy Ghost. I love God. I love my fellow man." But that is not the teaching of God. That is a shallow adulteration of divine truth brought down to the level of the human mind for mass consumption. And, in so doing, religion teaches man to violate the will of God.

To hate your life in this world is God's mystical code to tell you that you have another life, a divine life, a life not born in your mother's womb. "To keep your life unto life eternal" means that when you overcome your sense of a temporary human life that withers like grass and when you strive to live in your divine life now, the life that never withers, you will be reunited with the will of God in your Soul. And that act of will, will lift you into the glorious divine rhythm of your true self.

There are more than three hundred statements in the Bible that express the will of God for man. They've all been watered down, distorted, emasculated; and many have been forgotten. Sort of like toys that a child places in the closet when he grows weary of them.

Again, at the last supper, the will of God broke bread. And then to his disciples, who thought they were born of human flesh and blood, he passed the bread; and he gave them the secret of rebirth, "This bread," he said, "is my body; eat of my flesh."

Then he passed the chalice of wine, representing the divine wisdom, and said, "This is my blood; drink of my blood." Divine life was his flesh. The New Testament containing the wisdom and will of God was his blood. And also his voice in you was his blood. All his words and all his deeds were divine will in action made visible as a living testament to the truth that you are divine life and not human flesh.

To hate your life in this world is to live now in your divine life right here. To renounce the belief that you are human flesh is to accept the expressed will of God. "Whosoever eateth my flesh and drinketh my blood hath eternal life, and I will raise him up at the last day."

There you have the mystical secret of transition given to mankind by God. His flesh is your new divine life on earth. His blood is his divine wisdom and his divine will leading you, sustaining you, protecting you, nourishing you in every necessary way as you make the change in consciousness as you walk the path of faith and light.

And so when you say, "I don't know God's will," you realize that you are demanding that God speak to you before you are ready. Every divine word in the Bible is focused on one purpose:

To unite your mind and your Soul, to raise you to Soul level. This isn't attained by compromise, by mixing your human will and your divine will. Your human mind simply cannot receive divine blood direct. Your Soul is the channel for God's wisdom.

Automatically, the human mind adulterates; but the Soul delivers the pure thought of God. When you willingly lay down your human will and release the belief in the power of your human thought and strive to live your life at the Soul level, you are fulfilling what Jesus taught when he asked you to hate your life in this world; and you are obeying the will of God. And then you will be lifted from the mind universe in which man dies, to the Soul universe in which your divine Self lives.

The communication of God pouring through your Soul eliminates world thought, eliminates world images; and then you find yourself in the Father's house doing the Father's business. So when you learn to live at the Soul level, you will see that your light is shining; and you will never have to reincarnate again.

Let's turn off our tape recorders now and just be still a bit before we move into lesson number six.

∞∞∞∞∞∞∞∞∞ End of Side one ∞∞∞∞∞∞∞∞∞

LESSON 6: THE SECOND BAPTISM

Mystics like Joel and Bohme, who attained the second baptism, are able to live and move in the higher realm of the Soul because they did not ignore the will of God. They obeyed divine will, not only from the voice within themselves, but also when it expressed through divine messengers. If Joel had not obeyed the divine will expressed through the teaching of Jesus Christ, he would not have received the purple robe of Spirit.

And so, to all students who complain, "I don't know what God's will is for me even though I listen patiently," please correct that serious mistake. Divine messengers like Jesus bring the will of God to earth whenever they speak and wherever they speak and wherever they act. If you don't hear the voice within you, it probably is because you are ignoring the will of God as expressed by such lights as Jesus, John, Peter or Paul.

The words of Jesus were not his own, but the Father who sent him. First, Jesus came to his disciples with the will of God. Then he departed. When they learned how to live in their Souls, he returned. Now that's the sequence. First you obey the will of God brought by his messengers. That opens your Soul buds, and then you learn how to receive the will of God direct in your Soul.

So don't think your progress is hopeless or that God has no interest in you if your meditations do not yield God contact. Do what Joel and other students have done before you. Obey the statements of Jesus as if you had heard them direct, spoken by the voice within you. That's one of the big reasons why millions of sincere worshipers have not yet developed their Soul faculties. They didn't realize the price they were paying for ignoring such divine commands as, "He that hateth his life in this world will keep it until life eternal." And so they have been ignoring God's will, building a false sense of karma. The spirit and the sinner, the millionaire and the pauper all have the same basic purpose in life: To find their Soul and to find within their Soul the Will, Wisdom and Power of God.

Only your Soul can make the transition through death untouched, and only through your Soul can the glory of Christ enter your experience. Without your Soul, you remain a creature separated from the grace of God, seeking always but finding never. The missing link between your divine Self and your human mind and body is your Soul. Between your eternal life and your lifespan stands your Soul. Truly, your Soul is a strait gate to paradise. Unless you find it, the ravages of time will turn whatever you accumulate on earth into rust and corrosion.

It appears that we have freedom to choose. We can be housewives or accountants, administrators or sales executives, industrialists, educators, astronauts. We can win fame as artists and composers and writers. We can be praised by our peers, stouthearted citizens that we are, making our contribution to the human community. Yes, we can achieve all this without even fulfilling our life purpose. We can be everything we want to be and still be failures in the eyes of God. We can be healthy, comfortable, secure. But unless we fulfill our life purpose before we die, unless we open our Soul to the guidance of divine will, unless we permit our Soul to lead us out of this world into heaven on earth, we will be required to reincarnate in another physical sense of body; and we will have to try again to fulfill the life purpose that we have ignored. We cannot substitute our ambitions or our human will for the life purpose ordained by God.

The Word of God must be made flesh. You must bring your spiritual body into expression by living in it. The Word cannot remain unfulfilled. It cannot return void. It cannot be mocked either by the prince or the prostitute, the dictator or the do-gooder, the parliament of England or the Congress of the United States. Wherever the will of God is ignored, you are looking at a future corpse. And the sooner we learn that first and foremost, beyond all human goals, beyond all human needs, beyond all human desires, our only salvation lies in giving full priority to the will of God, the sooner we will break the stranglehold that imprisons us in tombs of clay called bodies of flesh.

It is the interplay of your Soul and divine will that guides your ascension into the many mansions of reality. Then, for you, the wheel of birth and death stops spinning. The doctor's cardiogram loses its potency. The rumors of nuclear war hold no terror. The instant you experience your mystical life, your mystical body not born in your mother's womb, you regain a glimpse of the glory you had with God before the world was; and for you the material world––which the Bible means when it says, "the tree of knowledge of good and evil"––no longer can feed its forbidden fruit to your mind.

Let's take a minute right now. Let's evaluate the degree to which you have been obeying or denying the will of God. Jesus said, "He that seeth me, seeth Him that sent me." Now how do you relate to that statement? Did you interpret it as the will of God speaking to you, telling you what to do? Or did you pass by like many millions have done? Most of us fail to connect such statements with the will of God. We see the words, but they do not seem to involve us or to make any demand upon us.

But now, remembering that whatever Jesus said is the will of God coming to you in such a way that it must change your life, your consciousness, and having a specific purpose relating to you, look again carefully at the same statement: "He that seeth me, seeth Him that sent me." At first it doesn't seem to get to the point, does it? And that's why we walk by, touching it superficially.

Now take another statement, this one by John: "In Him was life, and that life was the light of all men." Now put the two statements together, and the will of God will stand unveiled before your eyes.

- The life of Jesus is the life of God, statement number 1.
- The life of Jesus is the light of you, statement number 2.

Now if you're the light of God, the life of God, the self of God, and you continue acting like mortal flesh, are you not violating the will of God? Let's look again at those two statements.

"Thou seetht me, thou seeh Him who sent me."

And now John reveals "His life is the light of you." And here's the will of God through John and Jesus saying, "You are my divine eternal Son."

God is revealing your divinity, your present divinity. His life, your life are the same life. The Father of Jesus, your Father are the same Father. The one spiritual body is your body. And so divine will is saying there, if you are listening to the will of God expressed by the messengers of God, accept your divine self now and leave your mortal sense of body. If we do not recognize the will of God, naturally you're inclined to do your own human thing; and that is the same as violating the will of God.

The difficulty is that we had expected God to give us a list of things to do and not to do, but that is our human will predetermining how God ought to function. You see, divine will doesn't work the way we like it to. It often is dropped into our consciousness like a little seed, and we can let the seed die or we can nourish it until it yields its fruitage. When we're attentive and reverential to the will of God within ourselves, which declares that we are his life, not flesh and blood, then we must stop complaining. We can't be talking about earaches, backaches and heartaches. We have to wipe the frown from our faces. We have to send out the light of love and joy and laughter, sweetness, confidence, cooperation, compassion, consideration, peace, beauty, harmony. We impersonalize error. We impersonalize the opposite. We uphold the great truth, "Whoever seeth me, seeth Him that sent me."

I cannot be the light and the darkness. For in the light of God, which I am, there is no darkness. [birds chirp in the background] I love those birds, don't you? [continues] So who has the backache? Who has the earache? Who has the heartache? Who has the disease? Who is suffering the problems of this world? Only those individuals in the mind level of life, who believe in the concepts of their own mind more than they believe in the Word of God.

[speaking of the birds in the window] That little fellow's right out here looking in as we're doing our little thing here. [birds continue to chirp as Herb continues]

If you desire to live inside the will of God, you cannot accept a problem as belonging to you. You can accept no darkness in your light. And if something in you rebels and insists that you really have the problem, stop! Right there please, stop! You just doubled your problem. You see, you started with one problem. Now you have two problems. The thing disturbing you is your second problem. Your first and your biggest problem is that without realizing it, you distrust God. God says you are the light. Your mind says, "No, no; you are not the light." You believe that your mind knows more than God. And you insist that the physical evidence proves that you're right and God is wrong.

Why do you do this? Because your mind is trapped in the world mind. Many millions of wonderful people in this world are also trapped in the same predicament. They do not understand that the Bible contains the will of God. They do not hear the will of God telling them to surrender their human will to His will, to surrender their human minds to their Soul. They did not hear God tell them that flesh is grass, that the flesh profiteth nothing. To put on the garment of immortality now; to be transformed by the renewal of the Spirit of their mind. And so they remain in the human thought universe, and that's where they perish while the divine life they ignored always awaits them in their own Soul.

So please remember, the problem that bothers you never is the real problem. Look deeper. Every problem on the mind level changes on the Soul level. The crooked arm is seen straight. Abundance appears where lack seems to be. Wrong changes to right. Death changes to life. That is why God wills that you live in your Soul, where you can enjoy His creation without distortion.

Look at your hand; look at the palm. Hold it up in front of your face about six inches; look at it. Now move your fingers; wiggle them several times. Make a fist. Clench your fist once. Clench it again twice; unclench it; clench it; unclench it. Simple isn't it? It is for you. But think of how many thousands of persons there are in this world who cannot control the muscles of their hand to perform such a simple act. They have the same equipment as you have, but right now if their life depended on it they couldn't clench and unclench their fist. Some have Parkinson's disease, Parkinson's; some have rheumatism, rheumatic arthritis. Some cannot even hold a pencil or a fork to put food in their mouth. Some are paralyzed. Some are so weak that the effort of lifting food from a plate to their mouth would be unthinkable. Some have diseases that have restricted or eliminated their muscular coordination. And, of course, there are paraplegics who only have claws instead of hands.

What's the point of all this? Think. Ask yourself did God favor you over them? Did God give you hands that work and them hands that don't work? Did God give some people strong hearts and others weak hearts? Did God give people eyes that see and others eyes that don't see? Do you think God created idiots, imbeciles, mongoloids, stillborn babies, retarded defective babies? Do you really believe that God created babies with inherent tendencies to physical ailments from their mothers and fathers? Do you believe that God created the millions of human embryos who are aborted every year before they get a chance to breathe in this world? Do you believe that God created neurotics, psychotics, arsonists, rapists, psychopathic killers?

But where did they come from if they do not come from the one creator?6 Do you believe that God is punishing hundreds of millions of people with malignant cancer, heart disease, stroke, arthritis, diabetes and five hundred other diseases that destroy the human body? Then who created this body? Who created these diseases? Who created these human structures that are blotted out of existence by a single bullet, by a pair of faulty lungs or by a heart that refuses to beat? Who created the atoms of bullets and atom bombs? Is there a cue for us in this human carnage? Are we still calling these atrocities images and likenesses of God?

Are we still pretending that God created human flesh and then gave man a box of atoms and said, "Play with these, but don't make atom bombs and don't blow up the world?" Are we still accusing God of stupidity, of complicity in mass manslaughter and mass abortions? Are we still pointing a finger at God and saying, "You created all this; now show us how to survive?"

Or are we humble enough to place all of our human assumptions aside and listen to the voice of God saying, "Love not the world, neither the things that are in the world. If any man love the world, the love of the Father is not in him?" Is the creator telling us not to love His creation, or is the creator telling us that this world is not His creation? Do you still insist that God created this material world when God specifically declares that "My Kingdom is not of this world?"

Then remember this: If you seek the transforming experience of the second baptism, if you seek transition untouched by death, if you seek the spiritual power of grace guiding and fulfilling your life, you must start realizing that God is not the creator of anything that dies, whether it be a person, a flower, a tree or an elephant. The dream of a temporary life in a temporary body must be shattered in you if you wish not to reincarnate back into the dream. The experience of your spiritual self alive now in a spiritual universe now is the subject of our meditation before we move into the next lesson.

LESSON 7: HUMAN CONSCIOUSNESS

Reincarnation represents the failure of a human consciousness to find its own Soul and to continue its journey to the highest heaven, the highest level of consciousness. It makes absolutely no difference how successful you are humanly. You might be Nelson D. Rockefeller, public servant, industrialist, financier, philanthropist, patron of the arts, governor, vice president. You might contribute to the world on a scale unequal by few men and women, but you must return to this earth in another form if at the moment of death you're not living in your Soul. That's divine law. It's the manner in which infinity maintains the purity of the kingdom of reality.

Perhaps the greatest obstacle to attaining Soul consciousness is what the Bible calls flesh. That's why you hear about flesh so often in the Bible. When you see this word in the Old or the New Testament, immediately you think of the flesh of the human body.

But that's not right. Flesh, in the mystical code of the ancients, means the material universe. All matter is flesh. A tree is flesh. The earth is flesh. All the earth contains is flesh.

"He that soweth to the flesh shall of the flesh reap corruption." This, in simple language, means that whoever lives in a material universe must die. Religion living by the letter, not the Spirit, has limited the word flesh to human bodies, and then has perverted the Word of God still further by interpreting everything said about flesh as referring to sin.

The will of God teaches us to remember that Spirit, where matter seems to be, is the only reality. And so it tells us to sow to the Spirit which is there, not to the flesh which appears to be there. But again, religion rejects this will of God, refuses to see that God is declaring, *"This material universe is flesh. It is not My creation."* And instead of letting this divine revelation liberate man into the spiritual universe, religion enslaves itself and the human race in the grip of a mental concept called sinful flesh, implying that God created good flesh. None of this is true.

"Our real existence," says Joel—you'll find that on page 64 of *The Infinite Way*—"Our real existence is as Spirit, and only in the degree that we perceive our real existence as Spirit, do we drop the false sense of life as material. Then we see that the structural life of man, animal and plant is but the false sense of existence; that our concern for the so-called necessities of material living has been unnecessary; that although the beauties that we behold all hint at God's creation, they are not [repeat: they are not] that spiritual and perfect creation; that the sick, aging, dying appearances are not at all a part of real life. When we arrive at this state of consciousness, we begin to catch glimpses of eternal spiritual existence, untouched by material conditions of mortal thoughts."

There's another Biblical word for matter, and that's the word darkness. When Jesus declares, "Men love the darkness rather than light," he is revealing that the material world is our mental concept about the invisible light. That is why the mystic can look at the entire spectrum of human suffering, at all the catastrophes and atrocities, and know that the amazing truth behind all that we see is the invisible Spirit and not the appearance of these evils. The mystic knows that none of it is happening in the creation, but only in our mental re-concept about the creation. The light never suffers; only the concept suffers.

"Judge not according to the appearances." That's what the will of God says. Because the Light is always perfect. All imperfection lies in the eyes and in the five senses of the beholder. In other words, the incapacity of our mind to perceive the perfect light of God traps us. It tricks us into accepting our own mental misperception as reality. This world, which is not the Kingdom of God, is a misperception of the collective world mind. The evils of this world are all part of the group misperception, but so is the good. Divine light misperceived through the inadequate faculties of the human mind is the "glass darkly" mentioned by Paul, which Jesus called the "father of lies."

When God directs you to hate your life in this world, that's the will of God asking you to overcome your concept of matter as reality. And as you faithfully try to obey, gradually you will be lifted to Soul consciousness; and you will be released from the misperception of your human mind and of the world mind. God is teaching us spiritual evolution. Science teaches us human evolution on the material plane, a process that never rises out of the misperception of the human mind and always, always ends in death.

But God teaches us how to rise out of the death-producing wheel of material evolution by a new way of life, a new direction in which we develop our Soul capacities and trust the will of God to be our friend, counselor, provider, protector and sustainer while that Will guides us upward on the most fascinating experience known to man, the journey from man of earth to eternal Son of God.

It is not the will of God that you live a happy successful life and then die, or that you have three meals a day with butter maybe instead of margarine. The will of God is that you surrender your human will; that you worship God in Spirit not in flesh; that you transform from the body that dies to the body that lives; that you seek only the treasures of the kingdom, not of this world. In short, God says to you, *"Come home. I have sent you My messengers with truth, you can trust them. I have still more truth waiting for you at the Soul level to guide you all the way. Hear My Will. Obey My Will and follow the golden circle of your Soul to your Father's house."*

"Our goal..." Joel says in his chapter 'Our Real Existence' "is the attainment of spiritual harmony rather than a continuation in a material sense of existence with more ease or comfort....Spirit can never fail. Our task is to learn to relax and let our Soul express itself."

The golden circle of your Soul is the real secret of spiritual evolution. Every command of the Father, every expression of divine will is meant to prod you into that enchanted rhythm where Soul and mind move as one, so that your Soul can move beyond the earth experience in its return home. Only human ego stands in the way. Until your Soul subdues your human ego, it cannot complete its journey to paradise.

The voyage of your Soul through infinite consciousness consists of two undivided halves of one golden circle. The first half of the circle is called the descent from light into darkness or from day into night. At the start of its journey, your Soul is the infinite divine tree. At the midway or turning point, your Soul is the prodigal son, diminished now into a divine seed; and so it must now retrace its path and return to source to complete the golden circle and once more become the infinite divine tree. This return of your Soul is your rebirth, called the ascension from darkness to light or from night to day. Some also call it the path of illumination because your Soul must rely completely on its own divine light through each level of manifestation.

On the fourth level of manifestation, called earth, the birth of a baby is only the visible part of the invisible divine Soul bearing fruit. Until the mind of that baby is reunited with Soul, the journey of that individual Soul cannot be completed. Until the mind consciousness of the child becomes conscious of its own Soul and surrenders to it by uniting with it, it cannot manifest the light of God; and it blocks the growth of the divine seed which is striving to return home. The Soul remains a lost sheep that cannot enter into the sheepfold, and the mind remains asleep, stagnant. No matter how much human fruit it may bear or how successful it may appear to be, until the mind is baptized in the Soul by the Soul, the Soul cannot ascend from the night of earth into the day of heaven.

The seven days of Genesis, as you know, represent this golden journey of your Soul. Also, the six pots in which Jesus transformed the water into wine. Your Soul's return through the six water pots emerging as wine is the divine journey symbolized by both Moses and Jesus to inform you that it is the will of God that your Soul make this journey. And until your mind cooperates, your flesh and your Spirit are at war.

There is always divine communication between your divine life and your Soul. It's much more than a voice; it's Grace. It's the fullness of the infinite Godhead ever flowing through its own soul activity. That divine river of communication carries with it its own self-existent substance, its own Wisdom, Power and Will. It is always Omnipresent at full strength. It is God being God now and everywhere. Dominion lies in this divine river of substance. It is the unopposed miracle worker that maintains the eternal purity of the Kingdom of God. And there is only one place to look for it––right where you are. It is always where you are. It is in your room right now.

Some mystics have called it the eternal river of Love, because whoever touches it becomes Love; and all that is unlike this Love disappears. You may feel it in every word written by John.

Many non-believers felt it in the presence of Jesus, and they were converted just by the Love that flowed within (inaudible) when they beheld him. That same Love is always present in your Soul, waiting for your mind to step aside and let yourself be immersed in the invisible river within that is always eager to administer the second baptism to you and to anyone who is ready to serve the indwelling divine will.

Think for a moment of someone or something, some person or some object. Now in your mind see that person or object. See the image of that person or object clearly. You are creating an image in mind, consciously. That image is not the person or the object. It's a picture that you have created, and the substance of that picture is your thought. In other words, it's a thought image, a human thought image.

This actually is what you do all day. Only you don't do it consciously; you do it automatically. You create thought images in your mind. "There's John," you say, "there's Mary. There's a pepper tree, and there's a pussycat." The trouble with these images is that you do not control them. John can steal Mary's purse. Workmen can come and chop down the pepper tree against your will. The pussycat can run under the wheels of a car.

You see, all your mind can do is to record the changing images, just like a moving picture camera. But your dominion over these images is almost zero. That's because you are making automatic images without divine Love. You're interpreting the world around you through human thought because you inhabit a mind universe. Everything you experience comes into your mind to be recognized. Your reaction is so instantaneous you believe in the person or the object, but actually you are only seeing your thought about that person or object. You're seeing your own mental snapshots, and you do the same with all your five senses. You identify objects by your thoughts about them.

Now silently try to realize that the only thing you know about this world is what you think about it. Outside of your own thought you know nothing. Your thought is your world. The entire world is experienced by you as your thought in your mind. Now feel your thought. I mean feel it as the substance of this world. Feel your thought about anything. Think of the many unhappy thoughts that you have had during your lifetime, painful situations, errors in judgment, unpaid debts, accidents, sickness. Were any of these caused by divine Love?

Wherever divine Love is realized, there is fullness of joy. And so when painful situations, errors, unfortunate relationships, deaths, accidents and sickness enter your mind and become the substance of your thought, that is evidence of the absence of divine Love in your thought. Human thought is always separated from God even though divine Love is always present. But now let's take our camera and bring it in for repairs.

Quiet your mind, the thought substance in your mind; and let your thoughts drift into nothingness. Your Soul is the divine repair shop for the camera of your mind. Divine Love flowing from your Soul, the presence of divine Love warms your soul, restores your inner vision, changes the substance of your thought, restores peace for pain, assurance for doubt, supply for lack, hope for despair, wholeness for division.

What calmed the tempest when Jesus looked at it with his Soul? Divine Love through his Soul revealed the harmony that is always Omnipresent. Did the woman lose her leukemia when she touched the hem of his robe, or did divine Love radiate through his Soul revealing that God had never created leukemia? Can you see that the power of divine Love flooding through your Soul, infiltrating your mind, replaces human thought with perfect divine thought, dissolving illusory concepts and revealing the divine creation here, now?

What prevents this descent of spiritual power into your life? Only the separation of your mind from your soul. And what keeps your mind separated? False concepts. And the secret is that **all** material concepts are false concepts. Every material concept is another onion skin that separates you from the divine Love that flows only through your Soul. Each material concept you remove thins the veil.

And so between now and the next series of lessons, your assignment is to remove false concepts that are blocking the union of your mind and Soul, just as they are for most of the human race. Now here are some of the practices you will find very rewarding. Meditate on the following:

1. *You are not flesh and blood.*
2. *You are not human form.*
3. *The real Self of you is not living in a material world.*
4. *You are an infinite Soul.*
5. *The Will of God is here where you are, always.*

So that's our three lessons today. There's no room on the tape for four. And we do want to say that this Easter is probably going to be for all of us a different kind because we're not talking about resurrection. You are the resurrection. You are the living Spirit of God now, relaxing from the concept of a human self. And when Easter day moves into your experience, it should be in such a way that you can say, as Christ Jesus said, "Thou seeth me, thou seeth Him that sent me."

Much Love from the island of Kauai. Look for another tape in I guess about thirty days, and by the time October rolls around, we will have had seven of these tapes; and we will all be of one spiritual accord.

TAPE 3

LESSONS 8 - 11

Herb: From the island of Kauai greetings of the Spirit and Love to each dear friend who walks with us on this golden path of light.

LESSON 8: THERE ARE NO HUMAN BEINGS

Usually ideas beyond human understanding require thousands of years before they penetrate human consciousness. At one time the Holy Spirit declared to both Abraham and Moses,

"The place whereon thou standest is Holy Ground."

But, as you know, the magnitude of these divine words did not dawn on the human mind. It was unprepared to receive them. Again, this time through Jeremiah and Ezekiel, the Holy Spirit declared,

"I will make a new covenant with the house of Israel. I will put My law in their inward parts. I will give them one heart and one way. I will put a new Spirit within you. I will take the stoney heart out of their flesh and give them a heart of flesh."

This was a mystical code, again not understood by the human mind. It was introducing God's will into human consciousness, and this code holds the key for your salvation and my salvation and the salvation of mankind. It contains God's solution for the survival of every individual who walks this earth, God's solution for disease, for world starvation, for nuclear radioactivity, God's solution for the fires and floods and earthquakes and tornados and volcanos and every disaster that devastates our modern world.

So look closely at those passages if you will, Jeremiah chapter 31 verses 31-33, also chapter 32 verse 39, and then Ezekiel chapter 11 verses 19 and 20. Expose those verses to your Soul and you will discover a secret glory, a glory that Spirit offers to every single initiate who is dedicated to living on earth here and now as the divine Son of God. These words of God invite you and your fellowman to live now in your divine body, and *"I, the Holy Spirit of God, will walk inside you. I will abide with you. I will guide you. I will love you, protect you. I will be your eternal life."*

Now ask your self, how could God give mankind one heart? How could God take out the stoney heart of their flesh and then give them a heart of flesh? Had God made a mistake the first time? Had God given mankind a bad heart? Was God now going to give man a good heart? What is a stoney heart of flesh? And why was God replacing it with a heart of flesh?

Spirit was revealing and preparing the Soul of man to become aware of the divine body that is indestructible, eternal, immortal, ageless, timeless, your divine body, instead of the material sense of body, the human form we think we live in, which is not created by God and therefore not subject to the control of God. God was saying in those words "a new heart and a new way" that there is a body that is not subject to disease, not subject to disaster, suffering and death itself. God was saying,

"Nobody can be sick in a body created by God. Nobody can die in a body created by God."

All sickness and all death on earth occur only in bodies not created by God, bodies not controlled by God. Because God is the only power, therefore, whatever God does not control cannot have real existence. The idea was too vast, and it was too early in man's mental development for such spiritual ideas to have any specific meaning for the material-minded human race, but the seed was planted. Centuries later Paul unveiled the divine body of man not as a future event, not as something that would happen later in time, not something dependent on man's evolution. He revealed a divine body of man as a living fact, as the true reality of every man.

"Know ye not that ye are the temple of God? If any man defile the temple of God, him shall God destroy. For the temple of God is holy, which temple ye are."

Here was Paul revealing God's will, God's plan, that you live in your divine body, and also that by continuing to live in what you call your human body, you are violating the will of God and death is the inevitable result. When you do not live in your divine body, you are defiling the temple and you are separating yourself from divine life. What? "Know ye not that your body is the temple of the Holy Ghost, which is in you, which ye have of God, and ye are not your own?"

Again Paul reveals that if you are not receiving the Holy Ghost, it is because you are not living in the body that God gave you. You are living in your false concept of body.

A third time Paul repeats the secret truth. This time he adds a very special word to his message,

"Ye are the temple of the living God." As God has said, "I will dwell in them, I will walk in them, and I will be their God and they shall be My people. Wherefore, come out from among them and be ye separate," saith the Lord, "and touch not the unclean thing, and I will receive you and will be a Father unto you and you shall be My sons and daughters," saith the Lord Almighty.

Come out from among them who dwell in mortal bodies and be ye separate, and touch not the unclean thing. The unclean thing is our human concept of body. In other words, live in the temple of God. In all spiritual literature no words are more sacred or more misunderstood. Paul had learned the mighty secret of the Hebrew prophets. He had discovered that the separation between God and man is illusion. There is no God up there and no man down here. There is only God everywhere. Paul took God out of heaven, out of the sky, and he declared that the Spirit of God now walks this earth as the invisible body of every man.

He was two thousand years ahead of his time, two thousand years ahead of science and religion, presenting a truth so advanced, so staggering, that even today in the space age the human mind is still baffled by Paul's discovery. And the human body still suffers and dies, and man still believes God is up there and the human race down here. We still accept imperfect, defective human bodies of flesh as the creations of God. And in continuing to do so, we continue to defile the temple by ignoring and denying the presence of our own divine body, which is the Temple of God, which is the Creation of God, which is the Instrument of God, and which is as perfect and eternal as God.

Twenty centuries after Jesus and after Paul, the religions of the world still believe that God created the bodies of babies and then let millions of them starve to death or grow up to be gunned down on battlefields or to be ravaged by disease, disaster and other atrocities. We must take another look at ourselves. When Paul declares,

"He that soweth to the flesh shall of the flesh reap corruption."

He was alerting mankind that death can be avoided, that disease can be avoided, that suffering can be avoided by living in the divine body created by God. When he says,

"The letter killeth, but the Spirit giveth life,"

He is emphasizing that the grace and life of God only flow through the divine body of man. And finally, when he makes the incredible statement that there is neither male nor female, he is stating unequivocally that the physical body of male and female are both mental images, neither created, governed, maintained or sustained by the power of God. Paul is telling the world that God is not the creator of human bodies, and for two thousand years this truth has been too difficult for mankind to assimilate. Instead, we have accused God of creating defective bodies that die, vulnerable bodies that are helpless against the invasion of germs, deteriorating bodies that age and decay, hungry bodies that starve to death, and paralyzed bodies that have been mutilated and deprived of their life power. In declaring that God created them we are not worshipping God, we are worshipping a monster.

Today in this eighth lesson of our mystical series we are not turning away from the Holy Spirit, which spoke through the prophets, nor are we defiling the temple of God. We are not sowing to the flesh. We are not pretending that we can continue living in human bodies and under divine grace at the same time. And equally important, we are not going to ignore the words of a modern prophet who had the spiritual integrity and the divine ordination to step forward and to bring us face to face with truth that mankind has tried to avoid.

"There is no truth about a physical body because it is only a concept."

You'll find that statement on page 110 in "The Art of Spiritual Healing" by Joel Goldsmith. "There is no truth about a physical body because it is only a concept." And here's another,

"There are no human beings."

You'll find that statement on page 123 of Joel's book, "God The Substance of All Form." And here's another,

"My body has neither youth nor age. It is as ancient as God and as young as each new day."

That's on page 112 of "The Art of Spiritual Healing."

Today we're in the doing stage more than the talking stage. Today we are facing a truth whose time has come, that the human body is not the instrument or the creation of God, that the Son of God has a divine body, not a human body, that we have the responsibility and the power to live now in the divine body that God created, the body that never ages, that never suffers and never dies, under the grace of God, obedient to the expressed will of God, and independent of the material powers that govern human bodies.

Man has tried to worship God and has failed, because God must be worshipped in his temple and that temple is the divine body of man. To worship God while living in a human body not created by God is actually a separation from God. We cannot have two bodies, one Spirit and one matter, one divine and one human. We cannot be the opposite of what we are. We cannot reject our divine body without rejecting our own Self. We cannot live in a body that dies and live in our divine body at the same time.

All of these paradoxes and rejections of the divine will must be terminated if we wish to show forth the glory of God and to make the Word flesh. Only our divine body can bring forth divine manifestation. Only our divine body can be an instrument for God. And so it is, the dying to the human sense of body and the rebirth to the conscious experience of our divine body now constitutes our obedience and our dedication to the will of God. We practice the presence of God by practicing the presence of our divine body now. We no longer have a God up there and a me down here. We no longer make the Son of God a future event. We no longer honor a tomorrow God and a tomorrow Son of God by continuing to live in human bodies today.

What we have lived in for most of our lifespan is not our body but our sense of body. We've lived in bodies that become hungry, sick, but God made no such bodies. We've lived in mental images. We've lived in mental bodies governed by mental laws, not governed by divine law. We have not lived in our body, we have lived in our material sense of body. We thought that body and sense of body were one and the same, they are not. And now we are ready to correct our false concept of body and to enter into the new covenant. We are ready to enter into our mystical body which never dies. We are ready to enter the new heart. We are ready to enter our Soul realization of the mystical body. We are ready to know the truth about our real body which makes us free.

There are very specific and basic disciplines that we must practice in order to break material sense, and before we discuss these disciplines and apply them, it would be very beneficial I think if we listened to several important revelations about your mystical body that have been made by Joel.

"I," says Joel, "was here before I was conceived in my mother's womb," sound familiar?

"Do you not know that in our real identity that we are Melchizedek, having neither mother nor father?"

That statement is on page 113 "The Art of Spiritual Healing." Another,

"Mortals constitute the illusion. They constitute that which has no existence. How then is it possible to link a spiritual truth with that which has no existence? It cannot be done, do not try it. You cannot heal a human being, and I cannot heal a human being. If it could be done, God would have done it long before we attempted it. The sum and substance of the healing work is the realization, get this, 'the sum and substance of the healing work is the realization' that there are no human beings, that God is the only infinite being."

Please look at that on page 123 in Joel's book "God the Substance of All Form." And now let's go back to page 112 in the "Art of Spiritual Healing." A very key paragraph in your ongoing awareness of the divine body,

"My body," says Joel, "has neither qualities nor quantities of good or of evil. It has neither sickness nor health, is neither large nor small, has neither life nor death. My body is the temple of God, God substance expressed as form, embodying and including all the qualities and quantities which constitute God, the I-Am, the Soul. My body has neither youth nor age. It is as ancient as God and as young as each new day. My body is not governed by laws of matter or of mind, but by the grace of God, for Thine is the kingdom and the power and the glory. God is the light of my body. In my body is neither material darkness nor mental ignorance, for God is the light unto his holy temple, which my body is. God unfolds, discloses and reveals Himself as body, as temple, a place of holiness and peace. God's grace maintains and sustains His body, which my body is."

I would like now on that note, the acceptance that your body now is the divine body of God and that you have no physical body, you have one divine body, on that note let us be silent. Let us hold the truth, stabilizing it, and then as we become aware that we are accepting what God has been presenting to mankind since the so-called birth of man, let yourself rise even above human thought into the sacred place of the Most High, where there is no human thought, and rest there quietly.

Later you can come back to this same place, and later you can turn off your recorder at this point and just dwell in the knowledge of your divine body. But while you are resting there now, we will press on to the ninth lesson.

LESSON 9: LIVE IN YOUR MYSTICAL BODY

I really cannot stress or overstress the importance of what we are trying to do today. We wish to walk on hallowed ground. In a sense we are separating those who are dedicated and those who are not. We are saying,

"Henceforth, we who walk the path know no man after the flesh."

We are saying to those of you who have come this far and wish to go further that the next step is one of the most difficult you will ever take, but it is possible, and it is necessary if you wish to fully obey the will of God. Learning how to live in your mystical body which never ages and never dies is the secret of rebirth. It is also the secret of spiritual power, of grace, of freedom, and it is the secret of transition from man of earth to Son of God.

We will now concern ourselves in this lesson with the basic truths and the spiritual exercises that open your Soul faculties and lead to the consistent daily experience of your mystical body which is the true temple of God. You should realize perhaps that all spiritual healing takes place first in the mystical body and then appears as harmony or healing in what we call our physical body. It's the ability of the practitioner to live in the mystical body which is the secret of all absent healing. The reason is very simple and very astounding – there is only one mystical body.

When Jesus lived in his mystical body, he was automatically living in the mystical body of every patient whoever came to him. When a patient came to Jesus and entered his consciousness, that patient was actually entering his own mystical body. And so the contribution of Jesus was to stand in the secret place of the Most High, the mystical body which is the body of God and of man and of the human race, and to let the patient share the experience of the one divine mystical body, and that's why Jesus said,

"I of mine own self can do nothing. It's the Father within who doeth the works."

Now that's principle number one. Your mystical body and my mystical body are the same body. Your mystical body is infinite. It's the body of all who walk this earth and all who seemingly have passed from this earth and all who seemingly are still unborn. One infinite mystical body, which is the infinite body of God, is your true divine body now. That is why your mystical body never dies. But it is of very little value to you unless you live in it. Just as the perfection of your mystical body, when you're conscious of it, appears as healing in your physical body so do all the divine qualities of your mystical body, when you're conscious of it, appear as needed in your daily life. Children die of hunger, but not because of God's will, but because they are ignorant of God's will, which declares,

"You must live in your mystical body or you will destroy yourself."

Now this is divine law, call it hard truth if you will, but our ignorance of this law is responsible for all the unnecessary suffering on earth. Your divine body is the temple of God, and this is where the law of God is always functioning. When you do not abide in that temple daily, you are not under divine law, and that is the same as defiling the temple. You separate yourself from divine law and so you destroy yourself, and this is what Paul meant in 1st Corinthians chapter 3 verse 17, when he declared,

"If a man defile the Temple of God, him shall God destroy."

Once you know the law then the real discipline begins. If you stay in the temple, you're under the perfect God government. If you step out of the temple, you're under the government of the world mind, which as you know can tear you to pieces, invade your body with germs, drown you in a flood or cause your heart to stop beating.

This simple principle was so earth-shaking to King Solomon that he spent years building his magnificent temple as a symbol for mankind of the mystical body temple where man walks with God. When you live consciously in this invisible temple, you will be surprised to discover that the fire does not consume you, the bullets of the assassin do not touch you, nuclear fallout cannot contaminate you, germs cannot overpower you, and even crucifixion cannot kill you.

In this mystical body Jesus Christ remained alive during and after crucifixion of his visible form, and Enoch, the Hebrew patriarch, walked off the face of the earth into eternal life. In this mystical body the comatose girl recovered, the leper was cleansed and the storm became calm. In this mystical body loaves and fishes were distilled out of the invisible essence. If you believe in this mystical body, the work that Christ does you shall do, and even greater works shall you do, for the scope of your spiritual power is determined by the degree to which you fulfill or violate this irrevocable divine law.

Now let's get into the doing. Perhaps we'll have three, four or five meditations, one right after the other without a pause, and you will have to go back to these later to unscramble them and see the gem in each that you must make your own. But you want a rising continuity, and it begins right here, right now.

Really get rid of this world. Kick your shoes off if you feel like it. Get comfortable, relax. Get back there and be ready to give yourself away to your own divine body.

Many people try to get out of this physical body. Many teachings tell you how to roam in it and go places and return with a memory of what you saw. It's a lot of fun. It's not the Christ way. It's only partial, it's only fragmentary. In fact, it's an escape from the truth. The truth is that you can never get out of your physical body. Begin right there. You can never get out of your physical body because you never had one. You are not in your physical body now.

That right arm of yours, would you say that you're in your right arm? Suddenly, it will hit you that you're not there in that right arm. If they take that right arm away, you'll still be here won't you? Now try to see that just as you're not in your right arm, you're not in the body either. You really are not. This ageing body, this mental concept, is your sense of body. You are not in it. You are in your mystical body now, you have always been in it, you simply didn't know it. Rest now knowing,

"My divine body is present. It is here. It is my only body. I do not have two bodies, one that dies and another that lives. I have one body. It is divine, it is invisible, it is the creation of God, it is the body of God, it is my mystical body. I am resting in it now. I am coming out of the belief in physical bodies. I am free, I am unconfined. I am not a body of clay, I am Spirit. My body is not aging or dying. My body can never be sick or suffering. The only body God gave me is my divine body. When you see me, you see the Father."

"There is no physical person here." That is our step today. Are you taking that step? If your heart says, "Yes," we are moving into the recognition of our mystical body.

Where does your mystical body end? Nowhere. Where does it begin? Nowhere. Where is your mystical body? Wherever God is. I and the Father are one. Where is God? God is everywhere. Where is your mystical body? My mystical body is everywhere. It is a real body. The only body that exists, there is no other.

"My mystical body is the only body that ever will exist. It and the body of God are one and the same. I accept it. I am accepting the secret of the ages – the body of God and my body are one infinite, invisible, divine body."

Now I must learn to apply this to daily living. There's my neighbor and there's my neighbor's wife and there's my neighbor's son and there's my neighbor's dog. I see four or five different bodies, but there is only one divine body, one mystical body. It is my mystical body. It is my neighbor's mystical body.

Step number two – there are no physical bodies anywhere. There is only the one divine body of God, the mystical body of man.

Step number three – consciously remove all space between bodies. And this you will do later when your eyes are open, and we will discuss it now.

Make it a point for five days, and really you can't underestimate the importance of this. For five days, make it a point that whenever you see a group of people know that there is no space between their bodies and that there is no space between their bodies and your body. Do it consciously. When you see five people, dissolve the space between their bodies consciously and know that all that is there is the one invisible body of God, your mystical body, that joins you all in one mystical body, and unless you do this consciously, you will not be accepting your mystical body.

I have done this exercise. I have seen what it does. I have seen that within a short time, within less than the five days, you're looking everywhere and recognizing your invisible mystical body where people appear. And this is part of living in your mystical body.

Hold the silence.

Your mystical body is always the only body present no matter where you are, and while you are listening with your eyes closed, hear this from Joel,

"Every relationship in life is based on the belief that there are two or more of us. Two or more of us in the home. Two or more of us in the business. All spiritual truth, on the other hand, is based on the fact that there is only one I, one Consciousness, one Soul, one Spirit, and I am That I am. All that the Father hath is mine. All that is true of I is true of the Son." You'll find that on page 123, "God the Substance of All Form." And to Joel's statement you might add there is only one body.

And so we are now today declaring that I am going to remain conscious of my one infinite divine body, which is everywhere, and I am going to accept all truth that naturally is relevant to that basic truth. Because there is no other body than the one mystical body, my body is unopposed. Whatever appears that is unlike my one divine body must be an image in thought. And so we are saying that all of God's truth is functioning now in my one mystical body. All needs are already fulfilled. All truth is already complete. All that God is, I already am. I am resting in the one divine body of God, the one divine body of all who walk the earth, and I can face and will face every human problem with that knowledge – the knowledge of one body.

The opposite can never be true of divine truth. My one divine body, which is my only body, is neither young nor old, human or material, never imperfect, never temporary, never begins in time or ends in time, is never separate from itself, is never controlled by the world mind, is never incomplete, never lacks, is never under any material law. This one divine body is made of divine substance, activated by divine life, guided by divine intelligence, completely under divine law. This is my God body, my mystical body, my only body, always perfect, always functioning perfectly, always alive, always complete, always self-maintaining, always independent of material needs and material powers, always under grace, always manifesting divinity, always divinely controlled. And I can say as Paul did,

"I can do all things through Christ which strengtheneth me," because I have discovered my Christ body, my infinite divine body, which is always invincible, indestructible, unopposed, infinite, the one and only body of the universe. And all qualities that are not in my divine body are figments of the imagination.

That is only our first step. We are learning to stand in the truth that our divine body is here and not in our future, that our divine body is here and not in the sky, that the place whereon we stand is truly Holy ground because our holy body, our immortal body, our eternal body is now our only body.

Please practice these exercises individually, and then later you can run them together collectively as we just have done. Work with them, live with them. In five days of doing some of these things, you'll be astounded of how aware you are that you are not a physical form, and you will be prepared to receive higher levels of divine will. You will be prepared to perceive through your Soul what mortal man can never know.

"He that dwelleth in the secret place of the Most High shall abide under the shadow of the Almighty. A thousand shall fall at thy side and ten thousand at thy right hand, but it shall not come nigh thee. There shall no evil befall thee, neither shall any plague come nigh thy dwelling, for He shall give His angels charge over thee, to keep thee in all thy ways. Thou shalt tread upon the lion and adder, the young lion and dragon shall thou trample under thy feet, because He has set His Love upon thee. Therefore will I deliver him. I will set him on High. Because he hath known My name, he shall call upon Me and I will answer him. I will be with him in trouble, I will deliver him and shall honor him, with long life will I satisfy him and show him My salvation."

And so now we stand in the sanctuary of the Soul, the secret place of the Most High, resting in the sweet confidence of the one eternal presence with which I am forever one. For it is I, and I am That I am. Rest as long as you feel the descending peace of the Father, until that glorious hour when you truly experience the mystical body that is forever.

∞∞∞∞∞∞∞∞∞ End of Side One ∞∞∞∞∞∞∞∞∞∞

LESSON 10: THE WILL OF GOD

(tape starts abruptly) ...30 AD, about nineteen hundred and fifty years ago, a young band of Galileans were introduced to a new way of life. Their leader, you know, was an obscure carpenter from Nazareth born without a human father. Somehow his words touched their Souls in such a way that they felt these words had come direct from God. Of course, these men did not know that their leader was on earth to demonstrate the presence and power of the life of God in every man.

"Your human fathers taught you that righteousness is the way to salvation," he declared, "but I tell you that salvation is now in your own eternal life." His disciples were fascinated by these words. "I tell you," he continued, "it is the will of God that you be perfect as He is, for you are His eternal Son. It is the will of God that you live as a God man, a God man who never dies. It is the will of God that you be free from all false powers, that you be free from the powers of this material world, even that you be free from mortal flesh."

His disciples grew in number, of course, and as it did, his teaching became a little more difficult.

"When you live in the lower room of your mind," he taught them, "you're really blind, deaf and dumb. You live in a mind world, but not in the creation of God. You live in your own thoughts. You live in a thought universe separated from divine will, separated from divine law, and actually you are imprisoned in the world mind. But when you live in the upper room, which is your Soul, your light shines. Eternal life is bestowed upon you. The false powers of this world dissolve like morning dew and you walk through death untouched."

The disciples hardly dared to breathe for fear they might miss a single word. "I teach you no theories," he assured them, "for what I teach I personally have done, and what I do you will do. Even greater works will you do, for the life of God in you is a miracle worker without limitation. But remember this: Resist not evil. It is a trap of your mind. You can never find eternal life with that mind. Instead, enter ye at the straight gate. For wide is the gate of the mind, and broad is the way of the mind that leadeth to destruction. And many there be that go in that way because straight is the gate of the Soul and narrow is the way of the Soul which leadeth unto life, and few there be that find it."

At this time, while the young Galileans were following their Master, in nearby Jerusalem another man was studying the rules and rituals of Judaic law. Saul lived in his human will, in the will of his mind. He believed in matter. He believed in material good. He believed in material evil. He believed in material bodies. He believed that he was born in his mother's womb.

Saul was a Greek Jew, born in the city of Tarsus, and he had come to Jerusalem to study the traditions of his father. He very quickly distinguished himself in Judaism, winning the respect of the Pharisees for his high intelligence and for his total commitment to Judaism. He sat at the feet of Gamaliel, a great Hebrew teacher. He himself became a Pharisee, a defender of Judaic law, a man who regarded obedience to that law as the prime and sacred duty of every Jew. And Saul had another talent, a very important talent to the Pharisees. He could speak Greek, and many Greek-speaking Jews had joined the multitudes who were following the carpenter from Nazareth. The Nazarene movement had grown and now it included Jews and non-Jews drawn by the magic of his words and by his remarkable healings.

To the hot blood of Saul, any Jew who deserted Judaism to join this new heathen sect was a traitor and deserved nothing less than death itself. And so encouraged by many Pharisees and many Sadducees, Saul launched a vicious reign of violence and terror against every Greek Jew who had deserted Judaism to follow the new teaching of the Nazarene. So it was after the crucifixion and the resurrection of Jesus that Saul, determined to exterminate the early Christian movement that had infiltrated his native Greece, found himself on the road to Damascus accompanied by a band of hired assassins with one single-minded purpose: To kill every Greek Jew who had deserted Judaism to follow the new religion or way of life of the Nazarene.

To Saul's human mind this was God's will, that he wipe out these heathens. His human will substituted for the will of God had converted him into a fanatical persecutor and a killer of other Jews who wished to join the Christian movement. And at that point in his life, Saul was a symbol of the human mind and of the human race lost in the mind universe, violating the will of God, justifying its own human will by pretending it was the will of God.

And then suddenly, unexpectedly, the Soul of Saul replaced his mind. The mind universe disappeared. The physical world disappeared. The hate, the desire for vengeance all disappeared, and for Saul his own physical body disappeared. There was no Saul. There was no body. There was no world. He stood between two worlds totally blind.

Then he was directed to the street called Straight. The same straight gate Jesus had told his disciples was the only way to eternal life. The street called Straight represents the Soul of man. In this Soul the blind man regained his vision, but not his mind vision. New Soul vision opened for Saul, leading him to another universe where there are no human bodies, no human flesh to age, no human bodies to decay, no Christians to persecute. Dumbfounded, but ecstatic, he stayed outside his own human body in the Kingdom of God. The entire illusion of human life was shattered. He was no longer Saul born in his mother's womb. He was no longer flesh and blood; yet he was alive. In a way he could not have known with his limited human mind, he had been lifted out of humanhood, reborn into a spiritual being with a spiritual body and a life not dependent on human form. It was this amazing transformation in consciousness which opened his Soul to the will of God within himself, and in his dedication to that divine will within, Saul became Paul, the foremost Christian missionary to the Gentiles that our world has ever known.

"No man believed in flesh more than I did." That's what he wrote to the Philippians. "I was of the people of Israel. A Hebrew of the Hebrews. A believer in the total righteousness of the Pharisaic laws of conduct and of worship." Like most men he had believed that his life began with the physical union of his mother and his father. He believed that he was mortal, that he was born in the womb of his mother, that he was subject to the material laws of this world.

"But when it pleased God," he stated in another letter to the Galatians, "who separated me from my mother's womb." Remember that statement? "Come forth and be ye separate." Separate from your mother's womb, separate from the self you thought was born physically. "But when it pleased God, who separated me from my mother's womb and called me by his grace, to reveal his Son in me, that I might preach Him among the Gentiles, immediately I conferred not with flesh, not with blood: Neither went I up to Jerusalem to them which were apostles before me."

This passage in Paul's letter to the Galatians is chapter 1. It starts with verse 15, and really it contains one of the most electrifying statements in the history of man. And you will discover that there is no record that it has ever been understood by any theologian, any religious commentator or any religious leader in our world. The scope of Paul's discovery and its implications for the human race has lain dormant in the Bible because Paul's experience was too rare, was too extraordinary for any human mind to have any conception of his unique transformation in consciousness from matter to Spirit, from mind to Soul, from human body to divine mystical body.

So let's look at Paul's experience a little more closely. Inside his Soul he now saw the Son of God, and It was Himself. He saw his divine immortal eternal Self appearing now as a divine image. It is the same Self that he was before his mother and father were born.

It's the Self that he was before the world existed, the Self he always was and always would be; and It was real and It was present. It was Spirit. It could not be touched by human hands or by human weapons or by atomic fallout. It could not be contaminated by any disease or ravaged by any disaster. It could not grow old or weary. It could not grow hungry or poor. It was divine, with all that the word divine connotes. It was free forever, indestructible, self-existent, without boundaries in time and space. And most important of all, It was his only identity – his real permanent Self.

Paul had found the mystical body, and the physical self in which he had been living was revealed to him as a mental shadow of his own immortal body. That's why Saul was Saul no more. Forever after he would be known as Paul, for in finding his real invisible Self, Saul had been reborn of the Spirit. "When he was separated from his mother's womb" means he knew his true being, his true self, his true body which was not born of woman but of God.

Now this was precisely what Jesus has taught his disciples would happen if they believed in his teaching and followed the path of rebirth. This is precisely what happened to Paul, and make no mistake about it. When Paul said, "God revealed His Son in me," he was not saying, "I saw a vision of Jesus in my mind." He was announcing to mankind that in the splendor of Soul perception he had discovered that he himself was the living Spirit of God, he himself was the Christ and that he had never been flesh and blood.

No wonder he left Damascus without conferring with any man. No wonder he did not journey to Jerusalem to talk with the apostles. He had found his eternal life. From that day on Saul was Paul because the Christed man could take no orders from any man. The will of God within him became his leader, guide, teacher, protector, counselor and saviour. He was on fire. Paul had been anointed. He had been reborn. He had been transformed from man of earth to the living Spirit of God. His Soul now replaced his mind. Divine will replaced his human will. He had found the divine Self promised by the prophets of Israel and demonstrated by Christ Jesus. Within himself he found the saviour of mankind, the living Spirit that can wipe out war, disease and death from the blood-stained bodies of the human race.

And then suddenly to Paul the sacrament of bread and wine performed at the Lord's last supper now became a living symbol of the spiritual flesh and blood that he had perceived within his own Soul.

"Let every man eat and drink of that bread and that cup" he cried, because until you discern the true body of Spirit within you, your mystical body, you are weak, sickly and asleep. To Judaism breaking bread has been a symbol of heavenly manna received by the Jews in the wilderness during their exodus from Egypt. To Paul that bread now became the mystical symbol of man's spiritual body which could never die.

If we look at the 11th chapter of Corinthians, verses 22-30, Paul explains the mystical meaning of the Lord's last supper as the true basis of salvation, survival and of Christianity itself. Soul perception taught Paul that Christ, or Christos in the Greek language, is the real life, Spirit and Soul of everyone who walks the earth; of every Greek and of every Jew, of every freeman and of every slave, of every man and of every woman. He had been persecuting mortal flesh where only Christ stood.

And now, triumphantly, he announced, "There are two bodies, the natural and the spiritual. The natural body of flesh cannot inherit the Kingdom of God, only the spiritual can." The natural born body, born in the womb, he now knew incapable of fulfilling the will of God because it was not the creation of God. Only the spiritual body, the real body not born in the womb, could be a channel for God. This was his great discovery.

The invisible Christ life, the invisible Christ body of every man became the cornerstone of Paul's teaching, and with that teaching he walked spreading the Gospel of the invisible mystical body from city to city, fearing no man, accepting any persecution for the privilege of converting men from flesh to Spirit, from mind to Soul, from physical form to divine form.

"Be ye transformed by the renewal of the mind." That was his Gospel of faith.

"Stop believing what your eyes see. Stop believing that you're living inside human flesh. Stop believing that human flesh can fulfill the will of God."

Then in his letter to the Ephesians he amplified his meaning.

"Be renewed by the Spirit of your mind that ye put on the new man, which after God is created."

I think a more precise translator might have used the word Soul rather than Spirit of your mind, because Paul was revealing his stupendous discovery that your Soul is the vital key to transformation from your natural body to your mystical body, from hu-man to God-man. In fact, everything Jesus taught, Paul discovered was precisely true to the letter. And although Paul never took a lesson from Jesus in the flesh, he found the straight gate that leads to life eternal is the Soul, which he called that mind which was in Christ Jesus. Jesus taught it and Paul found it.

Every man has a never-born virgin life not conceived in his mother's womb. Jesus taught it, Paul found it. Every man who awakens from the dream of mortal flesh can live here now in their never-born mystical body. Jesus taught it. Paul proved that any man can do it. Jesus taught I am not in this form. You can crucify this form, and I will still be here alive. Paul, lifted out of the belief in physical form, discovered that when he had no form he was still here alive. Jesus proved it so that we may learn the truth about ourselves. And Paul, not crucified but visible, resurrected within himself, lived in his divine Self outside the appearance of form, obedient to the will of God within himself. And he did this by living in his Soul, which is the instrument for God which opens you to God's grace if you are willing to dedicate yourself here and now to living in your Soul, which alone can know your divine body.

Let's pause a minute and just hold the truth in consciousness.

There is a great transforming experience which you have either undergone or will undergo as you stand in your divine body. This transforming experience will take you beyond life in form into the Self that is always living outside form, and this is called your second baptism. Without this second baptism there is no Christianity or any other religion on earth. Because without second baptism, transformation through mystical rebirth, we are simply shells; and religion is a charade of ceremonies, rituals, rules, regulations, all making a mockery of the divine teaching recorded both in the Old and New Testaments of the Bible and in the great inspired scriptures of all true religion. Your second baptism experienced before death is the secret of eternal life. This transforming experience, taught by Jesus and even demonstrated in the life of Paul, is the will of God making visible to you the secret path to the Kingdom of God.

Jesus taught the will of God is planted in the midst of every man to lead him into his immortal life. Paul obeyed that will of God within him every day of his life after he discovered the truth after the blinding experience of Damascus. And though they never met in person, it is interesting to see that almost everything Jesus taught, Paul did. Everything that Jesus promised mankind, Paul experienced. And this amazing parallel in the lives of Jesus and Paul was the will of God demonstrating that truth is always true for every man, that the will of God in you is the pathway to the resurrection experience, the key to your transition.

They lived by the will of God. They taught that only obedience to the will of God can abolish death. They taught that the Soul is the only faculty which receives the will of God. They taught that the will of God is in your Soul. And as you dedicate yourself to living in the divine body, you will find that your Soul buds will open further and further and further. As you accept divine qualities here and now without opposite in spite of what you see, your Soul buds will still open further. And it is necessary, therefore, that you persuade yourself that only with Soul communication can you receive the will of God which enables you to enter the Kingdom of God, and that you must make this your number one priority.

It's necessary that we dwell on this subject even again and again and again until like Jesus, like Paul and like the disciples, and like all who have received their second baptism, we start each day by stepping out of our human bodies, out of our human will, out of our human mind, and resting; repeatedly making our surrender to our divine body, to the divine will, and to our Soul.

You should now in your early morning meditations live consciously in your divine body. Establish it. I tell you it is difficult. I tell you it is frustrating. I tell you it makes you want to find some other thing to do, some kind of respite from this effort because you're saying to yourself, "I'm trying to do it but I don't feel it." And I tell you forget your feeling. Forget everything except doing it.

And as you rest there with your divine body being your central thought of your entire consciousness; as you begin to feel a stirring of new life, of new being; as you begin to feel the presence of the Presence within you and then everywhere outside of that which you had called your body, you will realize that all of it everywhere is coming alive as you. It is your divine, everywhere body. It is a living force, and it will fill your consciousness beyond all doubt that the will of God is now present, functioning right there where your divine body is realized. And then, though you feel it not, though you hear it not, though you see it not, let it know itself in you; and that divine will in you expressing the will of God will guide your day as a living force. It will become the guiding force of your life.

The room doesn't have to fall in. Thunder doesn't have to peel across the heaven. The only sign you need is My Peace, that wondrous strange peace. And even if that doesn't come at first, even if you only see a pinpoint of light, or if there is a sudden click, a jerk, a jolt or whatever you want to call it. If your breath suddenly stops, if you feel a whiplash, and even if there's nothing at all, remember this: The truth is always there, and divine radar knows when you are making your surrender. Your human will will dissolve into the divine will of the Father who seeth in secret, who is always there, and it won't be long before you find there is a subtle divine rhythm which has taken over your life.

How many times you repeat this surrender of human will and human body to the ever-present divine will and divine body depends on your degree of dedication. Follow me. The more sensitive you are to this divine body and divine will, the more you will feel that God is communicating with you and through you. And the more you obey this communication instead of human needs, human desires, human will, human ambition, human goals, the more divine guidance you will receive. Daily surrender to your ever-present divine body, your ever-present divine life, your ever-present divine self, your ever-present divine will and all of your ever-present divine qualities. In this way you open your Soul consciously, and you prepare for the transforming experience which is called your second baptism.

Once more hold the silence. Know the presence. Reject all belief in a body that is not one with the body of God.

LESSON 11: WORLD WORK: WEATHER

Our eleventh lesson will be world work. I'd like to complement many of you who have already done your share of world work in your communities. Right now there is a rash of floods and all kinds of catastrophes sending homeowners running, and even in some areas they're shooting alligators and serpents with guns to keep them out of their homes. Some of you have done excellent work along this line in certain areas. Now it's time for all of us to know the great spiritual power that is in our mystical body. I prefer that you do not advertise this type of thing to students out of this work, please because we don't want people to start thinking of us as great miracle workers, but we do want to apply our awareness to community problems.

Now I think we would have to set a time that's favorable to everybody, and so 8 p.m. Pacific Coast time looks about the best. That is, every night after you receive this tape, for thirty consecutive days you're invited to join in a world work meditation. In California and Oregon, for example, you'll be meditating at 8 p.m.; and I suppose Chicago is two hours later, so in the midwest we'll be meditating at 10 p.m. Up there on the east coast you'll be meditating at 11 p.m. in New Hampshire or Massachusetts. And here in Hawaii we'll be meditating at 6 p.m. So that although we're on at different times according to the clock, we're all at the same time in our mystical body. Six in Hawaii, eight on the Pacific Coast, and I think it's probably nine then in Colorado and ten in Chicago, eleven New Hampshire and Massachusetts; and that's about the size of it. And we hope those in other cities can figure out the time that we're working on using 8 p.m. California or Pacific Coast time as your standard, so Alaska can figure out its own time. And we want to all be simultaneously involved in this work.

Now our subject is weather [spells] W E A T H E R, and in our work we do not have good weather and we do not have bad weather. All we have is the knowledge that wherever the world sees weather the world is seeing it through the sense mind. One day it'll see good weather with the sense mind. The next day it'll see bad weather, and millions would be homeless and helpless and running and fleeing from storms; and all of this, of course, is not the creation of God. We're past the point now of believing that God sends a flood to drown a village or an earthquake to shatter homes and lives or a volcano to bury a city alive. These things appear to happen, but now we are going to stand at the appointed hour not trying to stop the flood or the fire or the earthquake or the tornado, but knowing that where these things appear to be we are in our mystical body. Your mystical body is the subject of this meditation while the world dwells in the concept of weather, and through this you will see the power and the glory of divine law in operation.

Now let's see just how we would run through something like this. First I would say that during the day you should develop your understanding of this idea and know that God is not the creator of material weather. God is not the creator of anything material. Even though science thinks so or science thinks in some way that there is a God force that either operates this world or does not exist in this world, we are taking a different point of view. We are taking the point of view that neither science nor religion is aware that only a spiritual universe exists. That all that exists is your infinite mystical, divine, perfect, indestructible, harmonious body; and that everything within it is governed by perfect divine law. We are recognizing the power of God to maintain a perfect Kingdom at all times regardless of what the human eye may see. We are willing to rest in the Word. We are willing to stand in the secret place of the Most High. We know that if we keep our mind stayed on the truth, the peace of the Father will descend upon us and reveal the harmony of divine law.

Now then, as you practice during the day coming into agreement with these truths, you will be prepared when eight o'clock comes to enter the silence. You'll have many friends in Spirit with you, all of one accord.

Now let's assume that it's eight o'clock and we're ready, and we now go into the silence. We first establish that throughout time and space our mystical body exists and beyond. We do not see bodies; we do not see homeowners; we do not see farmers. We do not see physicality. We see one infinite spiritual body under divine law. We establish that. We rest there. We are knowing the truth. While we are doing this, the rain may be pouring in torrents at your window. Hundreds may be fleeing. Fires may be rampant. There may be predictions of an earthquake. Another storm may be brewing. A wind may be hovering off the coast. None of this is in your mystical body.

Your mystical body is infinite Spirit. All that is within It is under divine law and now in perfect harmony. There is nothing outside your mystical body. There is no place inside your body, and there is no outside to your body; and therefore, there is no place within or without where catastrophes can occur. There is no physicality in your infinite spiritual body which is unopposed. We are above sense deception. We are rising slowly to a place above mortal thought. We are recognizing that all mortal thought appears as the catastrophe that causes man to fear inclement weather. We are rising above the thought of a farmer that the frost will kill his crop, or the storm or the tornado. We are returning to our Father's house, the one infinite mystical body, the divine body of the divine son where I and the Father are one; and we are beyond mortal thought. Here we rest, and inside of a period of fifteen minutes we may attain our peace, our click, our awareness.

The first day may not produce that inner peace, nor the second nor the third, but we'll be there everyday for thirty days and everyday for fifteen minutes or more. And there will come a time when those of us who have not yet felt the quickening will feel it. And there will come a time when those of us who know the presence of the one power will feel deep within us that glorious peace that passeth all understanding. And our community will benefit, for the inner Christ will speak, and the earth will melt.

Now this is our assignment, and all who share our group purpose are invited to join. Unless you establish the infinite nature of your mystical body; unless you are willing to enter into that consciousness which recognizes that there are no human bodies, you will not find the peace, and spiritual power cannot flow. So if you must, during the day wrestle with the truth until you feel you know it that you may enter the eight o'clock meditation without the shadow of doubt.

I think that's clear now. And so with that we can now review the entire lesson from lesson 8 through 11, each day knowing a little more of what is being said. And hopefully, as the month progresses you and I will be standing together in the one infinite mystical body which is one with the Father.

For study you might read this month in the *Art of Spiritual Healing* the chapter "What about this Body," chapter 9. Then you might go on to chapter 11, which is about oneness. And I think you will find much strength in those chapters. Then if you want to go ahead of the class a bit, go into *God the Substance of All Form*, chapter 9, about individual consciousness. And you'll find that you are coming into the awareness, a strange awareness that the only inhabitant of the universe is You.

Much love from the island of Kauai. And we shall be as one all this month now in Spirit, in Self, in Soul, in our mystical body.

Aloha from the garden isle.

TAPE 4

LESSONS 12 - 15

Herb: From the island of Kauai, greetings of the Spirit to the Spirit.

I think I agree with you that we should continue our 8 p.m. meditations. And so everyday at 8 p.m. California time let us continue living in the mystical body, but let us change the subject. And if you will check the reverse side of this fourth tape, on the second half of it I think we'll do the meditation for the month, and our subject will be transportation: air, land and sea.

Another brief announcement about the seminar. It would be suggested to you now that you consider sending in your reservations before July 29th rather than wait, and the reason is that the inn at Avila Beach has given us a block of rooms for the students. But after July 29th those rooms that we have not reserved, they will start portioning out to other guests who may want to stay there. And also, if you do not plan to live at the Inn during the seminar, at least let us know that you are coming so that before July 29th we can set aside the required number of chairs. We don't want you to be disappointed, and we want to be prepared for you.

LESSON 12: GIVING UP THE BODY

Now today, because we are one, because we can be frank with each other and must be at all times, we're going to have to talk about things that are usually skipped for fear of offending anybody; and to me the greatest offense of all would be to bury the truth. So if it seems a little rough, it's what we all must do and what we all must face. We've got to learn to identify the excess baggage that stands in our way.

Your second birth is the secret of your progress, the secret that all great religions have taught, and the secret that many orthodox religions have refused to accept. Second birth removes the veil of illusions. It gives you a completely new universe to live in; a new body, new eyes, new ears, so that you can experience the eternal creation of God. Second birth lifts you right here into the Kingdom of God on earth. It takes you above the so-called material powers of the world, above human limitation; and you are no longer at the mercy of these strange world forces that have been beyond your control.

In this awakened realm you are released from the temporary sense of life. You are no longer bound by the temporary sense of body, and you are able to live consciously in your permanent self which automatically takes dominion over the elements of land, earth, air, fire, water, the powers of the world. This necessary evolution in consciousness brings you under a new law, a divine law, a perfect law; and it also eliminates all possibility of experiencing human death. While still appearing on earth you are transformed invisibly. You are made one in consciousness with the infinite Spirit, and you are governed by divine grace even before you make your ascension in consciousness out of this world because Spirit can read what is in your heart.

Some of you who are parents know that our parents as well as ourselves have been unaware that our true function on earth, as parents that is, is to teach the mystery of second birth to our children and to attain it for ourselves. As a result of this, most of the human race today, practically all of it, is victimized by death and conditions that lead to death. And although this transformation in consciousness has been attained throughout the world by many students of ancient mystery schools and has even been taught on earth for over twenty-five thousand years including a very special spiritual underground during the past sixteen centuries, in spite of all this, this world has been dominated visibly by religious doctrines that have distorted the truth. We have to face that.

The goodness of religion is not the goodness of God.

Our material sense has buried and has obscured divine truth, and the spiritual doctrine which we should have been learning has been confused with human doctrines, scientific doctrines, religious doctrines, all having ignored spiritual truth. And it was not until, oh, fourteen, say about a hundred and forty years ago, that the lost light was again rediscovered and the seeds of a new spiritual age were planted. Today you see them blossoming all around you with vigor, and it is now possible once more for modern man to break the hypnotism that has confined him to a temporary lifespan in a temporary imperfect body.

First birth is your birth into mortal form. Second birth is your birth into immortal life and immortal form, and that is the mystical path of illumination which fulfills the will of God, restores the lost years of the locusts and lifts you into the glorious realm of Christ consciousness.

You must have made the decision by now, and if necessary you must make it again and again every day, and that is this:

Are you Spirit or are you flesh?

Flesh is excess baggage. If you live as a fleshly organism, think as flesh, act as flesh, believe you and the world around you is made of flesh, you have accepted a temporary sense of life. You have accepted temporary pleasures, temporary security, temporary happiness. Your joys will be mingled with sorrows. Your successes in one direction will balance out by failures in other directions. And finally, all your possessions will be turned over to the probate court; and even the dear human body that you thought you were living in will be taken away. All you can take out of *this* world is your consciousness.

Life in flesh is responsible for every tragedy of human existence, for every up and down, for every gain and loss; and even while we're lifted up by a sense of progress, we find that our lives in the flesh are not really free. We're dominated. We're held down by physical forces beyond our control. Our bodies are vulnerable. At times our health is not stable. Our pressures and responsibilities multiply. Our energies diminish, and that proud unlimited vigor and enthusiasm of youth one day becomes punctured by a very sober realization that we're only beginning to repeat ourselves. We seem to have run out of options, and the newness of our lives loses its fine edge. We begin moving in grooves. We're held there by habit and necessity. Even our decisions are made for us by forces outside ourselves. And we may try to tell ourselves that we can conquer these forces, but we really know the truth; and it is that until we experience our permanent self, our permanent spiritual identity; until we evolve in consciousness from this temporary physical body to the mystical body of Spirit that never dies, no matter what we do or say, we remain prisoners of the flesh; and we try to survive by building mortal lives that we know must end.

Now that's the big sleep, and it's not for spiritual students.

Here are some more sobering facts on the excess baggage that we want to get rid of. During this next minute, one minute, one hundred and eight human bodies will die. I know it's not a desirable subject, but it's more desirable to remove the possibility of death. It's important to know that every hour sixty-five hundred human bodies die. Every day, *every day* one hundred and fifty-six thousand human bodies die.

Does it make you think a little bit about why?

And then here's the big one. In this year 1979 which we think is part of a great scientific age——the age of satellites, the space age——in this year of 1979 fifty-seven million human bodies will die. Again, in nineteen-eighty and each year thereafter another fifty-seven million human bodies will pay the same price. And you and I, having no control humanly, will simply wait around with the rest of them until we, too, become dead statistics unless we move into the second birth.

Perhaps it would help to know why we die from a different standpoint than medical opinion. Perhaps if we knew why we live under the constant fear of death, in the shadow of death and under the fear of physical conditions; if we could understand the why of it, we would have an opportunity of overcoming it. Why, for example, if God is life, why do human beings die? Do you know what Paul said about that?

He gave us an answer, a true answer, and was so shocking, so beyond the concept of the human mind that for the past nineteen centuries the mind of man has pretended that Paul never even said a word. Religions have actually put cotton in their ears. They have stuffed their ears so that they will not hear Paul's words. And you can say the same about educators and philosophers and scientists who have turned away, who prefer something less revolutionary, less disturbing than the truth. But Paul's words refuse to go away. And after every human scheme for survival or salvation has been tried and the death rate continues, we will discover that however shocking Paul's words may have been, they were not his words at all. They were heaven sent, and they were sent to lead us into our permanent self, where the experience of death is impossible.

"If you live in human flesh," said Paul in Romans 8, verse 15, "you must die."

Nobody wants to hear that, do they? We'd rather go right on living in human flesh and dying. But I tell you Paul knew of whereof he spoke, and if you look closely at his words––"if you live in human flesh you must die"––there's more there than meets the eye, because Paul is saying:

Number 1: That all human bodies, all human bodies, are separated from God. And this separation has nothing to do with your goodness or your badness, with your youth or your old age. Doesn't make a difference at all if a body belongs to a minister of a church or a member of the mafia. If it's a human body it will die. And death will always come under different disguises. But always behind the symptoms that cause death, there is only one true underlying cause; and Paul said it in this statement:

"The natural man"—–that means the natural human body—– "receiveth not the things of God."

Why doesn't the natural human body receive the life of God, the grace of God, the power, the love and even the protection of God? Why do a hundred and eight human bodies die every minute and fifty-seven million human bodies die every year? Face this now. It's important to your attainment of the second birth. The life of God is not in a human body, and the life of God does not animate a human body. The life of God does not sustain a human body, and all the religious prayers on earth cannot change these unalterable facts.

Maybe you never really realized it before, but today please do; and I think Joel is a good authority for us to follow at this point. And so let's take a peek at the book called *Spiritual Interpretation of Scripture*, page 211, that wonderful chapter called "The True Sense of the Universe."

"The secret," says Joel, "which has been so rarely understood is this: The life which you behold in man, tree or animal is not the life which is God. Human, animal or plant life is not a manifestation of God, and therefore is not immortal, eternal or spiritual. The life of material man or flower is mortal sense objectified. It is a false sense of life, a false sense of the life which is real."

Now that's the same as Paul's statements paraphrased another way. Do you really hear what Joel and Paul are saying? They are saying that the life of God is not in your human body, and they are saying that the life of God is not in the bodies of your children, and you cannot walk by on the other side. You've got to understand that and accept it. You've got to realize that because the life of God is not in your human body or in the bodies of your children, that those bodies are at the mercy of the false powers of this world. They are telling us why human hearts fail, why human brains suffer strokes, why human arteries harden and why all human bodies are not divinely governed. They are giving you priceless information that every human body on earth is separated from God until the second birth. And as a parent you must see that because of this truth, children are victimized by multiple sclerosis or muscular dystrophy only because their mortal bodies are separated from God. Now that's different from a scientific viewpoint or a religious viewpoint. That's a mystical viewpoint.

And the deeper meaning is that even healthy bodies are separated from God; that humanhood itself, living in a human body, constitutes separation from God. And that separation continues right up to the moment of death unless the individual conquers the illusion of flesh and attains the realization of his or her immortal permanent body, his mystical body, which is made of divine life substance that never dies. That's why we are emphasizing that you must find your mystical body and live in it instead of in your human body. And the facts may be blunt, but without these facts our entire human race has been paying the price of ignorance.

"While you are at home in the body," says Paul, "you are absent from the Lord."

Now what does "at home in" mean? It means while you are living in the body. And what does "absent from the Lord" mean? It means you are separated from God. Now that truth has been covered up. It has been covered up by ignorance in some form or another in the great minds of many of our leaders throughout the world. And literally that coverup has pulled a shroud over the face of mankind. It has veiled the light of God from billions of worshippers who thought they were living in bodies created by God, who are unaware that immortal Spirit, immortal God, cannot create mortal bodies of flesh; and that immortal Spirit, immortal God, cannot enter into mortal bodies of flesh.

This very day one thousand surgeons in this world will cut into one thousand human bodies to repair them, and why do these bodies need repair? Because God did not create them and because they are therefore separated from God. What God did not create is separated from God.

In Chicago why did two hundred and seventy-one bodies fall out of the sky and two or three more on the ground join in the carnage? Because they were separated from God. Not one of these bodies, not one of these minds in these bodies, knew how to be absent from the body; and therefore, they were not present with the Lord. And that's all it would have required. One passenger, just one aware of the infinite mystical body of Spirit would have made that DC10 safer than the lawn of the White House.

Every human disaster on earth reveals the truth that the body of man is separated from God. The body of the human race is separated from God. Every disease, every discord of a human body emphasizes this breach; and this is that big sleep. Blindly in our search for peace and survival we have ignored this immovable truth.

We pretend. We like to pretend that our bodies are images of God, that our bodies are created by God. We like to pretend that our human bodies can find the way to God. And we like to pretend that the power of God will lift us out of this chaos; out of confusion; out of hatred, fear, frustration, insecurity; out of war; out of radioactivity; out of terrorism and out of the moral irresponsibility that pervades many quarters of the globe. We like to think that the thousand conflicts that control man against his will will somehow be dissipated by divine power, that God will smile upon us and bless these human lives. But we are wrong. God cannot; God will not help a human being. Face it.

Those who are in the flesh, those who are in human bodies can never please God as long as they remain in human bodies. They can never even know God as long as they remain in human bodies, and they can never enter the Kingdom of God. This is Paul's statement to mankind. Every individual still living in a human body while declaring himself to be a born-again Christian is denying Paul's statement, is denying this mystical instruction by the founder of more Christian churches on earth than any other man. We actually perjure the words of God if we teach the untruth, and the untruth is that anyone living in the flesh can please God. For as Paul says, "As long as we are at home in the flesh, we are absent from the Lord."

And that's how Paul identified the universal problem of man, but he also identified the solution to this problem; and it was not a hearsay solution, an untested solution. It is, in fact, the only solution that works because it is a solution that pleases God. It is a solution that enables us to know God, whom to know aright is life eternal, not death. And so listen carefully again to what Paul says about the solution,

Awaken from mortality. Awaken from bodies of flesh. Awaken from bodies that die. Awaken from bodies that God did not create, bodies that God does not respect, bodies that can never walk in the creation of God or live under the grace of God. Rather, says Paul, "should we be willing to be absent from the body and present with the Lord."

Did you hear that word "willing?" If you are unwilling to be absent from the body, you will remain absent from God, absent from the powers of God, absent from the love and grace of God, the eternal life of God. But if you are willing, then be assured that you have passed one of the greatest hurdles to union with God. Your willingness to be out of the body, not for a minute, not for a day, but to consciously eliminate the concept of human flesh, enables you to move into the great adventure of finding your eternal, deathless, painless, perfect mystical body of Spirit.

Let's be still a moment before we move into lesson thirteen. Yes, that was twelve.

Let's just hold the quiet.

LESSON 13: SUMMARY OF HIGHER PRINCIPLES

I think at this point if we could stabilize and set down certain unchanging facts, then you could use these facts for meditation subjects. So in lesson thirteen, when you go over it, take these facts one by one and make them individual meditations. I may run them together into a group of meditations as we have done several times before, but I think you'll know exactly what to do. The important part is that there are certain ground rules which must be observed if we are going to live consciously outside physical form.

The first might be that no matter what you do, whether you live in physical form or not, there is an invisible you; and this invisible you is never going to die. It doesn't matter how much pain there is in the visible you. That pain is never in the invisible you. It doesn't matter if you find difficulties in this world; that if you are limited or lacking or unemployed or sick or divorced or whatever it might be, whatever upheaval comes, it's never functioning in your invisible self, your invisible life, your invisible body. That's fact number one, and so please make that the subject of a meditation. Get to know your invisible self.

You know how we are. We think of ourselves as minds and bodies, human organisms; and when you get through an entire day and look back at it, you find you've behaved like a human being. You've tried to find ways to bring pleasure to the body and to dodge pains that might come to the body, or problems; and you've moved in the sleep. You are not body! You are not mind!

You can see it better perhaps if you think of a rose bush putting out roses, and here's a dead rose now. You don't throw the rose bush away, and that's because you know that rose bush is going to put out more roses. In other words, you're not accepting the rose; you're accepting the life of the rose bush rather than the form of the rose. You enjoy the form of the rose, but you really are sowing to the life of the rose bush. You believe in it. You know that when the rose dies the life of the rose bush remains alive. And we want to go even deeper with ourselves – when this form dies, your life remains alive. And deeper still – your life that remains alive is the life of God. And that possibly is your second fact:

God Is Life.

But God is all life. There is no other life. Now a life that dies is not the life of God. When the life of your body dies that is not the life of God dying. And so if that's the life you're living in right now, you're living in the wrong life. That's not your life. The life of your body is not the life of God, but you are. Meditate on this:

The life of God is the life of you.

And your authority for that is the Christ teaching that the only life there is, is the life of God. "His life is the life of all men." You can thank John for that statement. Your life is the life of God, and even when the life of form is no more, your life is alive. So work until you are aware of the life of God as your life, and make the conversion so that you are living as the life of God and not as the life of this form. Until you do that you can see you're separated from the life of God, and in that separation from the life of God, because of a consciousness which believes in only the life of your form, everything that God is, is denied to you.

Just think if your blood was made of water instead of blood. Your body would need certain nutriments, and you couldn't get it out of water; you'd need blood. The life of God is your real blood. And if you're trying to live on water instead of blood, you have the cause of every human problem. Your God life is the only life there is, and the human sense of life is imitation. The light shining in the darkness is the life of God. It is your life, and it is eternal. It is unaffected by the things of this world. It is unaffected by inflation, unaffected by shortages, unaffected by discords and diseases. It is your life, though you may not have known it in your sleep. Awake from the sleep of a life that is not the life of God. Do not accept the life of this form as your life. That is the mystical truth number two that you must dwell with until you can shout it from the housetops:

"I and the Father are one life! The life of God, *I Am*! Thou couldest have no power over *Me*. You can only have power over the false sense of me!"

God is invisible. God life is invisible. Your God life is invisible, and it is always alive. And if you have heard those words within your heart, you will know that today, this moment, you can sit still and trust that invisible God life to function as you. It is your source. It is your source of all that you will ever need from now until eternity. It will never age. It will never weaken. It will never diminish. It is your true life. And it cannot work in you and for you if you are accepting the life of a human being. If you are separating yourself from it, you are living in that duality which brings about those one hundred and fifty-seven––what is it–– fifty-seven million deaths every year.

I tell you if you could walk up and down the hospitals of this world, and if you could be the consciousness of every person lying there knowing for them that the invisible life of God is their life, they would spring up. The dead would rise out of their graves. These mortality charts would be overturned. We would discover why we have suffered needlessly throughout the centuries confusing human life, a human blood stream with divine life and never knowing that the life of the rose that dies is still alive as the life of the rose bush. The life of this body that dies wasn't us. We are the life of God, the eternal rose bush ever giving life, ever sustaining life. We are not a dying rose; we are the Son of God.

God is immortal. God has no human body. The Son of God is immortal. The Son of God has no human body. Immortality begets immortality. Non-physicality never begets physicality. Your invisible life is God and also your invisible body. In order to experience your invisible life you must live in your invisible body. For the infinite life of God flows through your infinite invisible mystical body.

It is important to realize that your mortal life is only a sense of life and was not produced by the immortal life of God. It is important to know that the life substance of God did not produce your mortal body. Paul tells you that you have another body. You have a building of God not made with hands, eternal in the heavens. Not made with hands means not made of human flesh and not visible, not material. You have an invisible building of God. You have an invisible body, Paul is saying. And it is not temporary; it is eternal in the heavens. And where are the heavens? The heavens are your Christ consciousness. In your consciousness of truth you will discover you have an invisible body that lives forever, now. The life of God formed this invisible body, and that invisible life of God flows through this invisible body. You have an invisible self with an invisible body and an invisible life. And meditate upon this with the realization of fact number three:

You have no other self than this one invisible life body Self.

Do not make the error that you are both visible and invisible. There is no such you. You are not the visible body. You are not the life of that body. The visible life, the visible body, is not you because if it were, you would be separated from God. And therefore this comes to fact number four, a beautiful fact. Dwell on it until you can shout again, "Yes, I agree! I understand! I feel it!" And the fact is this:

The life that dies is never you. It cannot be! The life that dies is not the life of God. You *are* the life of God, and the life of God is always alive.

Don't wait to enjoy it five hundred years from now or ten years from now or twenty minutes from now. Acknowledge it in all your ways. Your invisible life and your invisible body are now alive and always will be. And this invisible life will always be your permanent divine source for everything you need. Just like the blood in your veins nourishes the body, your invisible life acknowledged, believed, lived in, accepted, worshipped, loved will be the substance invisibly of everything you need in the visible world.

I, your invisible life; I, your invisible body; I, your invisible Christ Self—I can never leave you. I am unlimited. I am completely unaffected by the conflicts of this world, and I am always here to remove those conflicts if you will but acknowledge Me as your life and not the life of the visible form.

As you daily learn to accept this invisible life, it will replace dying flesh, literally. And then as you extend this truth to your children, to all who live within the scope of your visible eyes, to every nation, and realize that the invisible life of one is also the invisible life of the other, you will be in the one invisible life; and that one invisible life is your saviour, your Self, the Life of all men, the Christ of the world. In Egypt, in Israel, in all of Africa, in England and in Ireland, wherever there are conflicts between men, it is because there is no one there to recognize, to live in, to experience the one invisible infinite life that flows perfectly sustaining the one invisible infinite mystical body of Spirit.

That doesn't mean that you're going to throw away this physical sense of life. You're going to see the human body in a different way, that's all. You're going to see it for what it really is. It's a guide, a measuring device. It's a map. You look at it, and it tells you the quality of your consciousness. It is a mirror of your consciousness. And in that mirror you see the conflicts, and they tell you that you are living in the wrong life.

If you didn't have this mirror, this map, this guide, this body to look at, you would never be able to locate your problem. But the minute the body shows forth some problem— whatever it is— whether it's in the body itself or its relationships with other people or the emotions that run through the body— whatever—your map is telling you get back to your consciousness. That's where it's coming from. And now when you get back to the consciousness, you find the secret: That consciousness is separated from God. It doesn't know God aright. It's a human consciousness. It's a sitting duck for world thought. It's reacting. It's hypnotized. It's actually asleep, and in its sleep it is dreaming because it cannot control the dream. And that's the value of your body. It brings you back to that consciousness which is sleeping and allowing the body to live in these conflicts. And when you get to transcend that consciousness by knowing that you are the life of God, that these things in the body are not yours; these temporary problems are not yours; this temporary body is not yours, you're not going to need it some day you know; and the sooner you learn that the only reason you have it is to help you purify your consciousness, the more grateful you will be for it and the more intelligently you will use it.

∞∞∞∞∞∞∞∞∞ End of Side One ∞∞∞∞∞∞∞∞∞

LESSON 14: TRANSFIGURATION AS TAUGHT BY JESUS

[tape starts abruptly] ...of this world. It doesn't make sense to anyone who knows the truth, and yet in spite of that, this is the prevailing assumption throughout the clerical world. And it is these incredible superstitions that have hardened into what is known today as religious doctrine, imprisoning men in minds and hearts and bodies not created by God, living in an atmosphere of fear and hate and ignorance with real truth hidden under a cloak of piety and at the same time completely losing sight of God's many statements that *His* creation is always perfect, that *His* creation is perfect forever.

Now that's where we begin in mysticism. That perfect creation is yours. That perfect creation is your sinless, painless, deathless, mystical body; and it doesn't have to be improved at all. It has never sinned. It has never lied. It has never cheated. It has never committed adultery. It does not have to be corrected or improved. It simply has to be lived in.

95

It was that mystical body of Moses that delivered hidden manna to the Israelites in the wilderness, and it was the mystical body of Enoch that enabled him to walk right off the earth and to leave no physical body behind him. It was a breathtaking glimpse of the mystical body of mankind that gave Abraham the courage and the confidence to bind his dear son Isaac, to place him on a pile of wood and to be ready to offer him as a burnt offering to God. As we take this from a material viewpoint, we lose it. But if we see it for what it was intended to say, as a dramatic symbol, as secret Spirit's way of teaching us that Abraham had reached the realization that God life is never in a mortal body; that's all it was saying. Spirit was demonstrating that in order to find your mystical body you must be willing to cast your material concept of body into the flame of Spirit.

Again, when Shadrach, Meshach and Abednego were cast into a fiery furnace, the prophet Daniel was revealing the mystical body of man, which can never be destroyed. And so a mysterious fourth man appeared in the fire, and the King said, "Who is this mysterious man? Why are these men still alive, and who is that fourth man?" And all the princes of the realm were assembled to see this great thing. Why did the fire have no power over the bodies of these men? Everybody was astonished. The hair on their heads was not even singed. Their coats were untouched, and there wasn't even the smell of smoke on them.

Very few now or then discovered the identity of that mysterious fourth man, and that is because the language of Spirit was not understood. We were looking through material eyes. We were not listening within. Spirit was teaching that the fourth man is the one invisible body in which Shadrach, Meshach and Abednego were living; the same mystical body that is destined to save all of us, all mankind, and to lead us safely through anything this world can offer, including nuclear radiation and including death itself. As we find that one mystical body, we walk the fiery furnace. We find the hidden manna. We find that we are not disturbed by the appearances of death that come upon us or seem to come upon our children. Rather, we stand in the one infinite divine life, the one infinite mystical body; and we see through the illusions of this world.

As a matter of fact, every healing in the Bible is an esoteric teaching that disease, disaster, discord and death are overcome by a transformation of consciousness from mortal body to mystical body, from visible life to invisible life. And we should also note that only after Jesus had revealed the mystical body of Lazarus was he ready to make the one great mystical body of himself visible to mankind. This was perhaps as extraordinary a demonstration as will ever appear on this earth, one of the great vital divine teachings in the history of all religions; and again, it has been dreadfully misconstrued by the sleeping clergy.

Look again and you find a teaching so powerful that it can change our present civilization. We have been taught by many that Jesus took John and Peter and James to the mount of transfiguration because they were the most prepared of all his disciples. Now there's another reason, even more important; and if you want to experience your own mystical body, you will have to have a better understanding of why Jesus took *these* three disciples.

John represents Love. Love without any form of condemnation. A Love that sees the Love of God even where the world sees evil. Pure Love without opposite.

Peter represents Faith. Faith in the power and presence of God. A faith, though, that is so great that even though Peter may not see God, even though God is invisible, that faith inspires deeds because Peter's faith in the invisible divine presence enabled him to become ultimately one of the great teachers of Christianity.

Now James represents Total Commitment. The commitment of your human selfhood totally out of the way, so that you can live in Spirit without opposite. And it was James who first sacrificed his human life, as you know, and became a martyr in the cause of Christianity.

Now these three qualities—**Love, Faith** to perform deeds of divine purity even without the evidence of a physical God or a presence of God, and then the **Commitment** to Spirit—these are your basic qualities, your basic equipment that enable you to move out of a dying body of mortal flesh into your immortal mystical body of eternal Spirit. So that's why James accompanied Peter and John, and the three of them witnessed on the mount of transfiguration one of the most important events in all religious history.

Years later, recalling that very spellbinding event, the Gospel writers told us that, "We beheld his glory. The glory as of the only begotten of the Father. His countenance was altered. His face did shine as the sun. His clothing became whiter than white. We were eyewitnesses of His majesty."

These are the phrases that have come down through the ages. And we ask ourselves, "Was that the whole story? Have we caught it? Have we understood why he charged them to tell no man what they had seen until the Son of man be risen again from the dead? Do we know what happened on that mount that could not be told until his resurrection from the dead?" Perhaps we can try at least to go deeper than the mere words.

Christ had awakened the three disciples from mortal sleep. He had lifted them above mortal sense, above material sense, above humanhood, above body consciousness; and now they were in Soul consciousness. They were seeing what eyes cannot see that look out from a human skull. They were seeing Soul pictures now, not mental images of the human mind; and with these Soul pictures instead of words, Christ was piercing the universal veil of illusion that has blinded man to the presence of eternal life.

It's as if he was saying, "Now open your inner eye. Look through the eye of the Soul. And now behold; behold the invisible creation of God."

You see, there were no longer three disciples there. There was the Soul standing looking into the three heavens. And there in the first heaven, the Soul of the disciples saw Elias, whom we also know as Elijah; and Elijah was alive. He wasn't dead at all. As John the Baptist he had been beheaded. But here he was, very much alive in the invisible divine life that is ever present. And also he had descended back into earth after he had once ascended as Elijah on a chariot. And so you see that Elias or Elijah could come and go, as they say, at will.

And then in the second heaven the Soul of the three disciples saw Moses, and here the Hebrew patriarch was very much alive; and they saw Moses and Elijah talking with Jesus. And Jesus was the one in the third heaven, but he wasn't Jesus anymore. He was no longer a physical body. Now he was Himself; he was the light of Spirit. He wasn't contained in a shape. He was the very atmosphere itself without boundaries.

Now in this Soul experience, the disciples of Love, Faith and Commitment did not realize that they had experienced and entered the mystical body of all who walk this earth. They were in the Christ body, whose substance is the very life of God. At that time they couldn't know that the life of this mystical body was the life of every man and woman who walks this earth. Nor could they even begin to suspect the eternal qualities of perfection that lay hidden in this invisible divine life ready to bless all who have the vision and the courage to overcome their false sense of mortal life in bodies of temporary flesh. And so Christ said to them, "Tell the vision to no man until the Son of man be risen from the dead."

Let us stand now on this mount of transfiguration and see the miracle of truth demonstrated for you that day. With human eyes they had seen Jesus. Now they were seeing one direct line moving back into the invisible. They were seeing that Jesus visibly was this invisible Self, which through Soul perception he was now permitting them to see. He was demonstrating his mystical body. It had no place where it began in space or time. It could have gone back endlessly. And it came now out of the invisible, slowly becoming perceptible, first as visible light and then finally as that which to some extent still resembled the man they had known as Jesus. All of that in one continuous motion without division, one.

Now put your face and your body in front of that light and see yourself in the visible as a visible form. And now let yourself go back into the invisible, further back until you are light; and now back into invisible light. Feel all of it, going back into infinity, disappearing into that which no one can see. Now come out of that invisible. You are the infinite invisible coming forth into visible light and finally into an appearance called man or woman, but all of it from the invisible out to the visible is you. In other words, when we look at you we see only the tip of the iceberg. We don't see your invisibility which is there. And so we look at your invisible, and we form this visible concept we call you. And you do it about yourself and everyone you know. Feel this infinite invisibility of your being, because that is what the mount of transfiguration was all about.

He was saying, "John, Peter, James; this is you. I am demonstrating your mystical body as well as my own." And as you rest there, as you feel the glory, as you know yourself to be the infinite invisible, you are opening yourself to the teaching of Christ that you are invisible life in an invisible body of Spirit. That you are eternal being right now, and that all this invisible universe here and now is you.

"Tell no man these things you have seen until the Son of man be risen again from the dead." It has another meaning, you see. When you know yourself to be that living Spirit, then the Son of man rises within you from the deadness of the mortal grave that we live in. You become alive with the Spirit, and the rising of the Son of man in you is your conscious realization of identity. And until it happens in you, what have you to tell?

"Tell no man until the Son of man is risen again in you." Then with that experience you can go forth living in your mystical body, trusting your invisible mystical life to go before you everywhere; and the light of your being will tell the world.

Only the crucifixion was the higher point in the demonstration of Christ. Lazarus was restored to his mystical body and could walk out of a tomb. The life had never died. The invisible life was always living. And immediately after this was demonstrated, the Master took his disciples to the mount to show them how it had been done. He had simply brought forth the invisible light body into the visible, and there was Lazarus again. He was saying, "Do it yourself." And then to show that nothing could take away that invisible light body, he said, "Crucify the physical form you see, and you will see that I'm still here. Destroy this body temple, and in three days I will still be right here showing you another body."

Why? Because those three days are the three heavens you just saw. That's where *I* live. In the fifth, sixth and seventh days of Genesis we find the three heavens, the three invisible worlds which are one world, which are your mystical body now.

I think we can move now into our fifteenth lesson.

LESSON 15: WORLD WORK: TRANSPORTATION

I think if you want to write me about some of your experiences this past month I would be very happy to learn what you went through. One woman wrote and said that on a trip to Texas on a plane, they were told by the pilot that for the next hundred miles there would be a great deal of turbulence and be prepared for it. They were going to go through it. They had no choice or they decided that was the thing to do, anyway. And so she went into her mystical body. She felt that she could not describe the joy of the experience because she wasn't in the plane at all, you know. And I won't tell you that the plane was in her either because she was beyond a plane. She was in her invisible life over those so-called hundred miles. She was alert. She had a companion, her husband. He too felt no turbulence. They didn't feel this rush of air you get when you came down. Nobody on the plane seemed to be aware of any turbulence; and when they landed, neither she nor her husband felt the contact with the earth. And the trip would not have been half as enjoyable if this pilot hadn't come through to tell them about the turbulence for a hundred miles ahead because it made them find their mystical bodies.

Now for the last thirty or forty days we've been working with weather. There was a great deal of work put on in certain areas, and hopefully we have had a successful series of meditations. At this particular point right now, from this moment or up to this moment, I'm not aware of any deaths that occurred because of weather conditions. I read about two in Indonesia, pardon me, from an earthquake. Two were killed about twenty days ago in Indonesia from an earthquake. But outside of that, even when I read about the fires, I read they were contained; and I looked and scanned each word in the print of the paper, who died, who died, who died. They never reported a death, and so I like to feel, and hope it's true, that together we have been instrumental in unseeing weather conditions. Certainly, we've learned a good deal; that we can be sure of.

Now we want to continue those eight o'clock meditations, and our subject is transportation: airplanes, automobiles, ships at sea, people swimming in the ocean. Now we want to learn how to do it correctly because in this world work it must be repeated again and again we are not trying to remove conditions. That's the best way to multiply them. And so catch this little trick of a technique, which is very important not only in these meditations but in your healing work. Perhaps I'll review it from a personal body standpoint so you get the idea more readily.

The person comes to you with a backache. They're moaning, and you love them. At least you want to get rid of it for them, and you've lost it right there.

Now let's look back at the lessons today. We were talking about the mystical body and the invisible mystical life. The life of God. And so you know that the life of God does not have a backache and the body of God does not have a backache and that God is all. God is all life. God is the only body. There is only one body. Now where are you going to get rid of a backache?

The minute you try to, you deny the allness of God, the allness of divine life, the allness of the one infinite mystical body of Spirit. You have come right under the hypnosis of matter. And now hypnotized by matter, you're going to try to remove the backache. You're right back seeing serpents in a tree in your backyard and trying to get rid of the serpents. And you can try all day. They won't leave the tree because they're not there.

You can't get rid of that backache because it's not there. Maybe someday you can tell that to the patient. Right now if you try to, they'll say, "Well then, why do I want to come to you for? If you can't get rid of my backache, I'll go to someone who can. There's a chiropractor who can do it, and there's someone else who can do it; and the medical profession knows all about how to handle backaches." And so tell no man. Someday you'll find there is somebody you can tell.

You can say, "Look, let's face it, you don't have arthritis. You think you have. You don't even have an ulcer. You think you have." Now you can't do that with most people, but there are some you can do it with and they listen to you; and don't be surprised that they finally agree with you that they don't have arthritis and don't have an ulcer. And it won't be because your mind is more powerful than theirs. It'll be because you have risen above the temptation to accept the appearance.

And you may be thinking, "Well, that's pretty superficial stuff. Wait until we get into brain tumors. Wait until we get into other malignancies in the body. You can't dismiss those by saying you don't have them." Yes, you can. God does. God is too pure to behold iniquity. Is the Son of God any different? There is one life and one body. And that mystical body is your body, and it is the body of your patient though the patient knows it not. And if you want to help, the only help you can give is to know the truth. That's first step number one on our transportation meditations.

Know the truth. Know the truth before the accidents. Know the truth that the life of God is not going to be in an accident. Know the truth that the life of God is all there is out there. That's all that's there. The life of God is where the plane seems to be with two hundred and seventy-three passengers. Only the life of God is there. Only the mystical body is there, with the life of God governing it. Know the truth that the life of God is where every driver of an automobile appears to be. There may be millions of cars on the road, but there is only one life; and you are the one who knows it. There is only one body, and you are the one who knows it; and that body can never be in an accident. That life can never smash up.

Now you're either in the mystical consciousness or the material consciousness. And during this month we want to see that the life of God is where the ocean is. And everybody can be running to the beach and into the higher waves, but only the life of God is there, only the one mystical body. And finally, it's the one mystical body in which this world appears to be; and it is your body. It is where the oceans are, where the sky is, where the automobiles are driving. And then when you're meditating during the July 4th weekend, by that time you should be ready, really in high gear rolling along, knowing the truth so well that your work should show forth in this visible world.

So let's go through a meditation or two. Let's catch the feeling. It's eight o'clock California time. Here in Hawaii we're back there at five o'clock now. Up there in New England you're up to eleven o'clock, I think, and so on out to Alaska and midwest and what not. We're all in the one mystical body governed by the one divine life. Now in your practice sessions, before you get into the July 4th weekend, take your thirteenth lesson of this tape and really fine-comb it. Know it so well that all of the principles mentioned there are put into practice in this meditation.

You're in the one invisible body. Just find your peace. Forget all the phrases. Forget all the truth you know. Find the peace of the one invisible body. "My peace I give unto you. My peace, not as the world giveth, I give unto you." There can be no death. We never heard of death. All we know is life. Life is all that is here. We are overcoming that last enemy, the last enemy called death. And now while we're doing that, let's go a step further. Let's see what John meant when he said that "The last enemy to be overcome is the second death." That's in Revelation, the second chapter. "He that overcometh shall not be hurt of the second death."

He had already disclosed that the eternal life of God is the life of all men, and you're knowing this now in this meditation. There aren't two kinds of life. There's only the life of God, which is the life of all men; and that's where you're living. The life of all men, whether they're driving a car or seated in a plane or swimming in an ocean. The life of all children, wherever they are. The life of this universe. The only life is the life of God. Find your peace in that. And if you don't find your peace in it, you have not accepted the truth of it.

What is that second death? The life Jesus Christ demonstrated by Jesus Christ is the life of every passenger on every plane, the life of every motorist driving a car, the life of every passenger in a car. All transportation–– air, land and sea––is an image in mind. We are living in the one invisible life, not in a moving vehicle.

Maybe the four billion on the earth have forgotten the divine life. Maybe all of us have, because when we came into mortal flesh we stepped out of our original divine life. We are all the one life and always have been. And then through mortal birth we departed from the consciousness of eternal life. That mortal birth became dead to spirit through a false consciousness. That is the first death. All human birth is the first death in the eyes of the mystic because it is a departure from the one eternal life. But we never did depart. We simply gave a sense of reality to a form, which we then continued to live in; and only when this form dies are we in the second death. John wanted us to know that. The first death he defined as human birth. The second death was the death of that which was born humanly.

So birth is death number one. The death of the mortal body is death number two, and we can avoid the second death. "If you become part of the first resurrection," says John, "you can avoid the second death." And that is what we want to do in this meditation for the world. We want to show that the second death is unnecessary. We're only using transportation as a way of demonstrating to ourselves and to the world silently that the knowledge of the one invisible divine life everywhere as your life and my life, accepted within, flowing now through your infinite invisible mystical body, is the only life out there. And when the glorious peace comes upon you, you are entering the first resurrection.

We're going to do this every night at eight o'clock through July 4th and beyond until you get the next tape, and we'll probably continue that so that we can have a different subject each month for our eight o'clock meditation, right up to the seminar.

Now then, let's look at John's statement a little closer. I think it's in Revelation 20 or 21. Yes, here it is; chapter 20, verse 6. "Blessed and holy *is* he that hath part in the first resurrection: on such the second death hath no power, but they shall be priests of God and of Christ ..."

As we rest in the one life, we are priests of God. We are the church of God. We are the living life of God. And something is happening within us silently, invisibly; changing the conditions of earth; removing the discords and disharmonies, the fears and the hates; making it impossible for this form to be guided by the world mind into those catastrophes that have engulfed the world.

Beyond our meditation as we practice this knowledge, something takes place within you day after day after day, a subtle transmutation replacing your false sense of body into a total oneness with the infinite in which your only body is that infinite body which appeared to the world as Christ Jesus, Christ John,

Christ Paul, Christ Moses. The infinite invisible body comes into a visible sense of body, but it is a one infinite continuity of body; and all is the invisible life of God; and the second death is overcome. This translation from the natural body to the divine is the evolution of consciousness that becomes visible as your divinely governed body, which for Enoch and others became the passport to eternity. We are no longer going to continue as bodies of clay subject to conditions of the world, not if we're willing to give up those sense bodies in exchange for the mystical body.

Now we have three more lessons; three more tapes, that is; and there'll be about ten or twelve more lessons on them; and their purpose will be to help you maintain the conscious continuous awareness so totally that even when you're not trying to think about it it's there. Just like you're conscious of air without being conscious of it, you know it's there. Just like your hands move on the brakes and your feet on the pedals of a car without really taking thought. So we learn the meaning of take no thought for your body; take no thought for your life. There will come a time when you won't have to take thought, a time when thought does its own thing and you *are* consciously only that body, only that life. Years and lifespans of habit as a human organism are thus erased from consciousness. The veil has lifted. Behold, the new Self emerges without the taint of a second consciousness, a second body, a second life.

Now these meditations on transportation are just as important for you as they are for those whom you are trying to walk with in the truth. And I think it's a good way to start your children off into this work a little higher than they have been. Let them meditate with you about transportation. Let them become conscious of the invisible life. Teach it to them. If necessary, tell them to tell no man. But let them enjoy this new vision of a life that never dies. Explain the difference between the life that never dies and the life of the body. They are less conditioned than you or I were, say thirty or forty years ago, or maybe twenty or ten years ago for some of us. They can understand more than we ever dreamed they can understand. And you'll see that our work on transportation has many important ramifications for you, your family and mankind.

Thirteenth lesson is a summary of the higher principles that you must practice. The twelfth lesson is a giving up of the body. The fourteenth lesson is transfiguration taught by Jesus to his three disciples, taught by Jesus to all disciples throughout the world who bring forth Love, Faith and Commitment; and taught by you to those who come within the perimeter of your consciousness whether they know you or not.

Be still and know I in the midst of you, I who can never leave you, I who go before you, I who make all the crooked places straight. I am your infinite divine life, and I function through your infinite mystical body of Spirit.

And you will discover the first resurrection taking place within you, that elevation of consciousness which dissolves the experience called the second death.

Much Love from Kauai. We'll see you again in about thirty days as we join again in oneness of the Soul. Much Love.

TAPE 5

LESSONS 16 – 19

Herb: From the island of Kauai, once more we come to you with the Spirit of Love.

We've had fruitful meditations at 8 p.m. California time, so please continue those meditations. Our subject starting immediately will be energy, divine energy; and I believe that later, probably in the second half of the second side of this tape, we will discuss the technique to use over the month in those meditations.

LESSON 16: THE SEVEN STEPS

We've come a long way in only fifteen lessons. This is the sixteenth, and it is the fifth tape. And we want now to proceed into the high mystery of transformation. We're all acquainted with Paul's statement about transformation: "Be ye transformed by the renewing of the mind." And there's an unfortunate word in that translation: the renewing of the "mind." And so we've all been content to dwell at the "mind" level of transformation.

We should be reminded that Paul made several other statements about the same subject. One of them in Colossians chapter 3, verse 10, is this: "Be renewed in knowledge after the image of Him that created you." And there the transformation then is turned to "the image of Him that created you."

And again, another way of referring to the same subject was made by Paul in Ephesians 4, verse 23. "Be ye transformed by the renewing of your mind" is not exactly what he had in mind because he said now, "Be renewed in the Spirit of your mind."

And so these new ideas that should be included are the Spirit of your mind and in the image of Him that created you. And you will see that these give your work on transformation an entirely different meaning, a new depth and a new weapon for spiritual progress.

It is very clear now that transformation is not possible when you continue to live in the idea that you are a material person and that you are now living in a material body. Perhaps you were not quite aware of it during your monthly meditations, but whatever success you had in meditating this past month was made possible by your willingness to release your sense of body.

If you read the instructions or hear the instructions again before each of the meditation series and feel the flux of where we were going, you will see that you were being led out of the belief in form, out of the belief that you are living in form, and into the knowledge that you now are the living Spirit of God.

And in order to prepare for the higher mystery of transformation, let us now renew our acquaintance with our spiritual Self. Let us be still. Let us return to that which is the image and likeness of God, the divine son who is not confined, who cannot find a material body to call his own, who has no place to put his head. That Self, that Infinite Spirit, I Am. This was the Consciousness that many of us brought to the 8 p.m. meditation.

Today we're going to share several important discoveries made through the ages pertaining to transformation. We're going to learn that when we say, "The Spirit of God will quicken your mortal body," what is meant is that you will realize you are not in a mortal body. That the Spirit of God will quicken your consciousness of your reality so that you recognize that the only body you have is the infinite mystical body of Spirit. This is the level that we are now trying to capture, to retain, and to work from, not only in our meditations but in our daily life.

I am that Spirit which is the Spirit of God. That is who I am and I am no other.

If you will recall our meditations on weather, you may have noticed that there was a very sharp decline in all of the disasters that were appearing in our country and abroad too. There was always a rash of hurricanes and fires and floods and earthquakes, and at the time we began our 8 p.m. meditations, these were really erupting all over the country. And then as you began to get into consciousness and we worked together, somehow these abated. You could open a paper at night. You wouldn't see anything in them about disasters, and you'd wake up in the morning and open your morning paper and again no floods, no fires.

Surely, after thirty days of that and a complete absence of disasters all across the country, you must have realized that you were part of a living group consciousness that was not in a form but was a living Spirit, containing the power of Spirit. And in various parts of the country there were different types of fruition from this activity. Someone up in Texas told me about the greatest crop in a twenty-five-year period because of very specially good weather.

Now while we were developing this group consciousness we were not flowing with the tide of world thought. The main part of our technique was that we were willing to make an adjustment in consciousness before we entered the silence, and then when we made that adjustment and entered the silence, our new consciousness of truth, of Spirit, of the present perfection of God everywhere, appeared as that truth in the visible.

Finally we moved into transportation, applying the same principles: That only God was present, that there really were no individual automobile drivers. Only God was present. And in that we were standing in our mystical body.

When July 4th rolled around there was a different power coming through the transparency which we call our group consciousness, and articles came in to me from some parts of the country stating that on one entire day there was not a single fatality over the July 4th weekend. And there were further reports that there had been certain estimates made about the number of fatalities, and again in certain areas the estimates turned out to be almost one hundred percent higher than the actual fatalities on the road, so that throughout the country we really shattered all records. It wasn't just a case of in one city there were no fatalities, but rather that maybe forty-five percent of the normal fatalities over July 4th were eliminated. Of course, we could say gas shortages were responsible for a large part of it. But again, because of our experience with weather and then moving into transportation, we could also feel that shortages did not account for all of the reduction in driving fatalities so that many so-called human lives were saved.

As a matter of fact, we came to a point where we were very confident of ourselves. We had reached a sort of a peak, a pinnacle; and it was at that moment that something very unusual happened. We were on this upswing. We were all feeling a new confidence. We were all feeling some power that we knew was there because of our new consciousness, and at that moment Skylab entered the world consciousness as a threat. It may not seem that way at this moment, but just a few moments ago, you know, Cincinnati wanted to put a roof over the whole city; and other areas of this country were wondering what are we going to do? Where are we going to hide? There's a seventy-seven-ton monster plunging through the sky. And everybody who could read a paper or turn on a television set was saying to themselves I feel a little fidgety, not very comfortable. But here we were, and the series of so-called coincidences had occurred so that at this very moment when Skylab threatened the world, we were at the peak level of a meditation on transportation in the air, on the land and in the sea. How could we ask for more?

I feel that you and I were part of something that we should remember for a long time whenever we feel a little indecisive or uncertain about the power of Spirit. I think you and I can say that we participated in an important spiritual event. And I think we should be reassured that when the city of Perth, Australia, who received the full brunt of Skylab's reentry, was able to say that since Skylab reentered the earth, fell into the sea, there has not been one injury or any damage from the largest man-made object that ever crashed out of space.

I want to congratulate you and everyone of you who participated in this event with the idea that because of it you should now be feeling that it is possible to do things that hitherto may have seemed impossible. And also to know that we are being prepared for a very special mission. Something far greater than bringing Skylab back to earth. Something far greater than moving out into the sky on a satellite or a space colony––something called transition. And in order to achieve this pinnacle of spiritual power, it is necessary to keep working on such projects as this until our confidence in the power of Spirit within us is so great that we find it possible to join with the scripture which says, "You can move mountains."

That was a mountain, that Skylab. And you know, it was strangely a fulfillment of a prophecy in an almost literal way. If you look at Mark, I think it's chapter 10. No, chapter 11. Mark 11, verse 23. Listen. It's really funny:

"For verily I say unto you, That whosoever shall say unto this mountain be thou removed and be thou cast into the sea; and shall not doubt in his heart, but shall believe that those things which he saith shall come to pass; he shall have whatsoever he saith."

Well, our mountain called Skylab fell into the sea. And for me it strengthens that divine proof that together, you and I, are learning something vital about Christ, something vital about our life, our spirit and our Soul. And that the resources of our own divine Christhood are truly available on earth now as they are in heaven.

Perhaps that will give you further confidence that when Spirit says, "Whoever will accept Christ identity will do the greater works," you can feel certain that there must be a plan now functioning which can help you witness the mystery of these greater works. You will discover that Spirit is calling your Soul, preparing you, inviting you to the mystical marriage. Releasing your Soul to the immaculate conception, the divine consummation called your second birth, which eventuates in your conscious realization of divine individuality.

You, I, every member of our group, and everyone who touches the consciousness of those who are moving into spiritual reality will be lifted out of lifespans, out of spans of living that end. Out of bodies of dust, bodies that return to the ground. Out of bodies that are subject to contamination by disease and decay. Out of false boundaries of space and time, shattering the veil of separation between us as mortal beings and our reality as divine being.

If you can stand back in consciousness and catch a vision of the lie and the truth, it may be important to you in the great work that lies ahead. The vision I have in mind is the truth of being, the spiritual universe, the invisible Kingdom of God. The pure light of being that is omnipresent everywhere now; pure, pure divine light. No one can remove it. No one can influence it. No one can make it impure. No one can adulterate it in any way.

The Kingdom of God on earth is here. It has no opposite. It is perfect now, and all it contains is its own perfection maintained perpetually unto eternity, under divine law, under grace. Always in harmony, always functioning flawlessly; always self-existent, self-fulfilling. That is the Kingdom, and that is where you live. The You that lives in that Kingdom now, in the invisible here, is real, perfect, eternal and is called the Son of God, the image and likeness of God, your divine individuality; and all that God is, your divine individuality is now.

And over all this is the veil, the density hiding the truth of the invisible self that you are. And in front of the truth stands this image, a form that is temporary, a form that has been unable to remove the injustices of the world, the fears, the uncertainties, the temporary nature of human life. And that form, that image, must learn how to pierce the veil, must learn how to bring forth out of the invisible the perfection that is here. And so you may call that a transformation, and you may say, "Well then, how can I bring out of the invisible that which is here? What is the plan? What is the process? You mean I can remove all my limitations and all my struggles? Can I overcome disasters and diseases?"

And the answer is that as long as you remain as the image of form you have no real validity as being. You have a dying substance and nothing more. You have a mind which is separated from the infinite divine mind. You have a heartbeat that must stop someday. And as long as your life is spent trying to protect this human image, you are giving away your life. You are removing yourself from your own identity, your own being.

And so "be ye renewed in the Spirit of your mind." Enter the invisible. For as you enter, the separation of your human sense of self from your divine true being will be dissolved. The upper worlds––which are your true selfhood––and the lower worlds––which are your false selfhood––will then be one world, one universe, one being; and you will be awakened from the sleep of a material self that never was.

That is why we have been working to build confidence in your own spiritual power, so that you will know that this spiritual power could only emanate from your Spirit. We are breaking centuries of reincarnating cycles of mortality. We are breaking the scientific illusion that being the most intelligent species on earth is our identity. We are breaking illusions that we are made of bodies of atomic dust that is both temporary and imperfect. We are breaking the illusion of a body that we must defend against our fellow man, of a body that must fight disease and of a mind that hopes for a better world. We are not hoping; we are knowing. We are not seeking; we are accepting. We are not asking; we are living in that world now.

And as we stand in this awareness of identity outside of body, not only shall **we** awaken, but the human mind of our fellow men shall light up like a million stars; and the reality behind the veil of matter will stir in the consciousness of man. He will be led as we are being led to dissolve the mist of matter; to push back the walls of his mind; to become a citizen of the infinite invisible, the limitless creation; to peel off onion skin after onion skin of mortality and to walk as the living Son of the living God.

Because you and I are now willing to commit ourselves to spiritual life in a spiritual universe under only spiritual law, every silent yearning in our hearts begins to be answered by the Spirit. And Spirit itself moves the mountain of doubt into the sea. The path of the invisible opens up from the very deepest reservoir of being. You become aware that there is a divine plan for you, for every individual on this earth. And that is when the secret of transition wells up deep in your consciousness and tells you that you can walk out of the changing cycles of death and birth, death and birth, into the life that never ends.

Today we want to get acquainted with seven steps, seven very unusual steps—the steps to immortality. And strangely enough, these steps can be called the T.R.'s, the path of the T.R.'s, because every step begins with a word that begins with T.R. Truth is the key, divine truth. And this is the truth that is going to take you into your conscious awareness of immortality.

Now how are you going to find this truth? Where is it? It's all around you, but it doesn't have a form that you can see. What faculty are you going to use to find it? You tried with your mind. We've all repeated the words. We've quoted Christ. Our world isn't that much better because of it. No. It's not the kind of truth you can use with your lips or with your memory. It's not the kind of truth that you can store away in your mind and pull out when you need it and expect the words to have a great power. Words didn't bring Skylab back safely or improve the weather. You're going to have to transcend your mind.

And that's your second T.R. And by transcending your mind you must come above all material concept. Up, up, up, up, up over every belief that matter is here; that matter has power; that matter shapes your destiny. That if you don't have a certain kind of matter you have no supply. That a certain kind of matter can go wrong and your digestion doesn't work. That a certain kind of matter can form a lump. We're coming above those concepts. Transcending the mind means releasing all material belief, because the mind is the prison in which we believe that there is possibly a spiritual universe behind the material one, but this one is here and this one we must deal with now. Out with all that thought if you want truth.

Transcend to your Soul. In your Soul, your single eye will perceive no experience. The universe of the Soul, which is not material, which is behind the material appearance; you will feel another living consciousness there. You will be indoctrinated into your permanent consciousness. You will rest in the Word. And because the Word is invisible, because the truth you are seeking cannot be found with the human five senses, you will think perhaps that you are not making the contact. But as you transcend mind and Soul is released from the prison of mind, if you are now prepared to become a transparency for that truth, you will be into the third T.R.

Transcending the mind, we stand in Soul, receiving truth through the Soul; and our Soul becomes a transparency through which divine truth will reach our consciousness. The words of Christ spoken in the Bible and the words of Christ that no one has ever heard will be speaking inaudibly and sometimes audibly through your Soul and through the mind, which is now surrendered, that it, too, may become a transparency for divine truth. And this invisible flow, this flow of living waters is the new substance for your transformation of consciousness, the fourth T.R. There is a conscious effort in the first T.R., the second T.R. and the third T.R. By the time you reach the fourth, there is no conscious effort. There is no taking thought. You are now entering the period of Grace.

From this point on, the entire flow of truth through the transparency of your Soul now flows into a new consciousness, reshaping, reforming, transforming. This new consciousness opens the vast inner resources of your being. And while you are in this transforming consciousness, there is a twin action taking place called transmutation. The transformed consciousness is now transmuting your old sense of body into the divine image and likeness of the Father, and you become aware of another body, another heart, another life. There is a transmutation taking place by grace, brought into operation by your transforming consciousness, all the way from truth to transmutation. This is all an automatic process.

And as you maintain the flow of truth through your transparent Soul, the transformation continues and the transmutation continues until you walk this earth in your mystical body, free of your visible body, the living Son of God; which leads you to the sixth T.R., your transition. That is the path you will take if you seek out truth; become obedient to it; let it do it's divine work within you. And you will find that your direction is different than the human race, and that the evils or so-called evils of this world drop away from you, because the moment you are in the transforming consciousness you're in the power. And when you're in the transmuted sense of body, which is now the body of pure light, the everywhereness of your being, you're beyond disease, beyond disasters; and the world will still be looking at what they think is your physical self. This is the path of transmutation by grace, which leads to the only transition there is—transition out of the false sense of the world into the permanent divine creation and the permanent eternal life.

Perhaps you'll desire to return for some unfinished business. Perhaps that's your mission, and you can; and so you can re-enter this world. And there are some who re-enter this world and make the seventh T.R., a translation, which is a special kind of transition. For in translation, like Enoch, like Jesus, the world can never find your physical body. You say, "I, the Spirit of God, never had one." And your conscious knowledge of this removes even the image of a physical body. There simply is no one left to bury.

The seven T.R.'s. They are already working in you. And please know that nothing can prevent the perfect activity of transformation, transmutation and transition if you remain faithful to your human function, your mortal function of overcoming the sense of good and evil, opposites, good and bad, health that is good one day and bad another day, and overcome all of these positive/negatives that oppose each other, because they have no existence in Truth. Your loyalty to truth is the trigger that sets in motion the path to transition. And when you step out of that loyalty, you step out of the possibility of attaining your transition.

We will intensify our understanding of these factors in lesson seventeen that follows this after you hold the silence just a wee bit longer.

LESSON 17: TRANSMUTATION

The mystery of transmutation is in your Bible, but the word is never used; and so the world has passed by. You will find transmutation revealed in a very special sequence, and only for those who had the level of consciousness that was ready for transmutation did this become apparent.

The girl in a coma, the twelve-year-old girl, was suffering from a mysterious ailment. What was the mysterious ailment? Sleeping sickness? No, that was not it. She was the first step. She was being transformed in consciousness, and that was leading to the second step, which was the boy who was in a coffin in the village of Nain. When he released his Soul to truth, it led to the place where within himself he died to mortality; and this is the outer visible evidence.

First, the transformation, which was the girl of twelve in a coma. Second, the death of personal self as personal self is transmuted into the awareness of divine self. And third, Lazarus coming out of the tomb. Transformation of consciousness and transmutation of body have led to transition. And these three progressive steps are all a visible demonstration by the Spirit of what takes place within you. You will find your human consciousness becomes comatose. Your human consciousness is placed in a coffin, and a new you emerges from the tomb of physical form.

This has not been explained to traditional religions because the level they are working at is not the same as the level of transition. And I hope at this point that all of us are prepared to surrender all desire to simply improve a human lifespan and to devote our attention to what man calls the practical ways of life, because it is very practical to let your transformed consciousness envelope you in safety and your transmuted consciousness multiply your supply and send you through the jaws of death untouched. I consider this more practical than anything that we can do on a human basis. And remember that nothing you do on a spiritual basis makes it necessary for you to overlook any human responsibility because the Father who seeth in secret knows every need, and the secret of Spirit is that it is always self-fulfilling.

Now sometime during this month please, you yourself go back to those three events: The girl in the coma; the boy in a coffin at the village of Nain, and Lazarus entombed and freed from the tomb. And read this from the Soul level knowing this is a secret way of telling you that these are inner activities of your dying sense of mortality and your borning sense of immortality. They are actually symbols of processes that actually take place within your consciousness, unseen to the world, if you are living in divine truth.

And when you read those episodes, don't think you're finished until you have found the central core of each episode so well that you can sit back and plant it in your consciousness and let it be the leaven of your new awareness. Meditate when you have found the central theme of each of these three episodes. Be still with that central theme, and you will see that all three episodes will synchronize in your consciousness to form their own kind of transformation and transmutation.

You'll find that you will be guided to these passages in the New Testament. No one will have to tell you the chapter and the verse. And if your search for them takes a little more time than just a second, all the better, because in passing you will discover other things in scripture speaking to you instantly about the invisible process which leads to transition.

And now let us enter the consciousness of the comatose girl. We are asleep to this world, but we are awakening to My Kingdom. And soon something in us is dead to this world. Our old sense of life is in a coffin, but we are awake in the invisible Kingdom of God here and now. And now our old sense of life is buried in a tomb, but we are still here. We come forth the new man. Maybe they'll say that's the carpenter's son, but will it be? Will not the new man be the Christ that you always were, free of the mortal sense of life, yet appearing in the mortal world while you walk consciously in the Kingdom?

Be sure to check those passages. Be sure to meditate upon them, for it will help you help yourself into the pure light of being.

∞∞∞∞∞∞∞∞∞∞ End of Side One ∞∞∞∞∞∞∞∞∞∞

LESSON 18: NO POWER

(tape starts abruptly) ... has ever existed in you unrecognized. It was with you before the world was, and It is with you now, ready to perform all the miracles of old, just as It has for all of the dedicated Souls who have walked this earth. It declares to you something that you must listen to, something that all the great ones have listened to. It says to you, "Without me, you can do nothing."

And if you have not heard that within yourself and if you do not believe that, listen again. "Without the living Word in the midst of you, you can do nothing." For it was the living Word in Jesus that said, "I am the way." The living Word is the way. "I am the door." The living Word is the door. "I alone can show you how to make the Word flesh," that you may dwell forever in the house of reality.

You see, Jesus was a transparency for the living Word, for Christ, for the Spirit of God, the same living Word that is in all men who walk the earth today. And it was this living Word which was the source of all the amazing powers displayed by all the prophets, all the great seers, all the great healers, all the great doers, all the great miracle workers.

"My doctrine," said Jesus, "is not my own. If I speak of myself, I bear witness to a lie. Why callest thou me good? There's none good but one." That one is the living Word. The living Word has come a light unto the world. Whoever believeth in the Word shall not abide in darkness. That Word is the power of your being from on high directing the image that walks this earth. As the branch cannot bear fruit except it abide in the vine, no more can ye except ye abide in the living Word, which has come that ye might have life, divine life, life more abundantly than you have ever known.

And just as Jesus could say, "I can do nothing. The Word of the Father within me doeth the works," so those who are dedicated to truth learn that their guide on the journey is the truth that God has planted in the midst of each of us; and to this truth, like Jesus and Moses and others, we become a transparency, a transparency for Christ.

This is our opportunity and our responsibility, and if we throw it away, we die. If we accept it, the miracle of the living Word leads us successfully through transformation of consciousness, transmutation of body and transition into my Father's house of eternal life. That living Word is now in God, and God is now in that living Word; and this is the way to your eternal freedom. "Of mine own self I can do nothing." The miracle comes back into your life when you step aside, when you become a transparency for Christ; and then the living Word does it all for you automatically.

Think for a moment of the first commandment. "Thou shall love the Lord thy God with all thy heart, thy soul and thy mind." How many people on earth are obeying that commandment to love God with their Soul? We have forgotten. We have ignored that commandment. We have ignored the divine command to love God with our Soul, and we have lost divine truth.

Today the human race is looking for energy. It is here. The human race is seeking peace. It is here. The human race seeks survival. It is here. It is just beyond the point of separation where man ignores the living Word. That Word is truth. That truth is alive. That truth is of God, and it flows; and it can take you and your loved ones out of dying bodies because that truth, that living Word, is a substance. It is the very substance of God, the life of God; and with that substance your transforming consciousness transmutes you into your mystical undying body and ultimately into your eternal selfhood.

And that is why the living Word is so important for this world. It is the only link between God and man. And every divine command has one secret purpose, and that is to move you into the invisible, to open and develop your Soul faculties, to make you a transparency for living truth so that you can individualize the perfect eternal qualities of God right here.

We have made a grave mistake in believing that a human being can take us into a higher level of consciousness called the divine Christ consciousness. It cannot be done. There is no human capacity to transmute or to make transition. Only your Soul, which transcends the human world and the human mind, has the capacity to love God and to receive truth from God; and only as this divine truth, this divine food, filters into your consciousness can the grace and the power of transformation and transmutation prepare you for the greater works which Jesus assured you, you will do.

There are many persons on earth who are very careful about the food they eat. They watch their calories and their cholesterol. They build one area of their body, and they decrease in another area of their body; and the spiritual student learns to be just as discriminating about the food that he permits to enter his mind. And finally when the spiritual student understands the direct relationship between truth and transformation, he realizes that without the truth of God as his only food, he is really starving his Soul; and he is pushing away the Kingdom of God right out of his life.

Now this knowledge is going to be firm in you, and when it is, God will become your only authority, your only source for truth. Then you will really be on the path of transition to your eternal life, the path that removes you from the veil of illusion. And you will have the only power that can trigger and sustain the invisible process of transformation and transmutation. You will do this by transcending your mind, letting your Soul be a transparency for the living waters of divine truth and for the meat that the unillumined world knows not of.

Now there'll be some who tell you they know all about transmutation. The physicist, for example. He sees transmutation as a physical event. He tells you that the nuclear structure of uranium, for example, disintegrates; and then it transmutes to other elements, Plutonium and radium. Fine, that's true. The botanist has an equal knowledge of transmutation in the world of nature. He sees sunshine, water and minerals transmuted by a tree into leaves, flowers, fruit; and that's what transmutation is to him. The entomologist sees the earthworm, and then he sees it transmuted into a butterfly. And the biologist tells you that there's a transmutation in the womb of a pregnant woman; that the fetus transmutes through the various phases of its lower evolution. All true. Just as true as the dreams of the alchemist who would like to transmute baser metals into gold and silver. But all this, all this, is not mystical transmutation.

The mystical transmutation is from the human sense of body to the eternal body of Spirit. It's a transmutation from mortal man of earth to immortal Christ of the divine Kingdom. And this transmutation from man to Christ is your mission on earth, and when it becomes your number one priority, you will not fulfill human needs through your manual efforts, but by grace. You will not lack and find human limitations, for you will have found the Kingdom in which all things are added. And you will fulfill the will of God that you be reunited with God in consciousness, and you will no longer be a separated individual living in that long parade of human dualities that manifest in our confused world today.

You can stop all dualities, all division. You can rely totally for every human need on the living Word to be present, to be active, to be alive, to be all powerful; and you can refuse to give power to world conditions and bodily conditions, and you can accept only the power of divine truth. When you do that, when that is your priority, you will be loving God with your Soul.

Now in Joel's teaching that is called the principle of no power, and that is why today we must learn this principle so well that we make possible the entrance of the living Word into our consciousness. Because as long as you are giving power to the lie, the truth of God cannot activate and transform your consciousness. In the thirty or thirty-two or -four books that are on the market by Joel today, there isn't a place where you cannot look at an index and find the principle of no power. It is so important that he has repeated it dozens and dozens of times. And there are still some of us today who are living without that principle. That principle says, "Seek no God power. Just open your Soul. Accept no limitations. Just open your Soul. Son, all I have is thine."

Don't wait for Christ to be born. Christ already is born in you. Just open your Soul. Give no power to man, to place or to thing. Give no power to good or to evil. Give no power to employment or unemployment, wealth or poverty, justice or injustice. Fear no loss; it will be restored. Fear no disaster; it cannot touch your divine life. Fear no power on this earth, not even nuclear power. But in your love of God as the only power, in your love of the presence of God as the only presence; you, too, individually can move the mountain. Because your name already is written in heaven. You can count on it. The Kingdom of God already is within you. You can count on it.

And the moment you draw your sword to resist evil, you are saying to the tempter I believe *you;* I don't believe God. I believe the picture confronting me. I don't believe the perfection of God is assured by the invisible presence of God. And in that instant of duality you have lost the power of no power. The moment that you accept the presence of the lump, the sin, the disease, the threat of disaster, you are in duality. You are denying the infinity of spirit. You are straying from divine truth. You are separating yourself from source. You are crawling back into the tomb of flesh. You are overlooking the principle taught when the twelve-year-old girl through the power of transformation of consciousness came back into a body that worked. When the young man in the coffin through the transmutation of body came back out of seeming death into what is called life. When Lazarus in a transmuted mystical body walked back into our world to teach us that the transparency for Christ who receives the living invisible present Word of God never remains in the tomb. If you do not receive the living Word of God, you are refusing to love God supremely. You are acknowledging devil power. You are accepting the opposites to God, who has no opposites; and you are really shutting the door of your Soul to eternal life.

Now let's reverse it. Let's stop every temptation from the outer world. Let's trust the power of the invisible living Word to be within us, to be on the job twenty-four hours a day, to be maintaining our perfection in spite of whatever our eyes see. That's not too big a job for us, is it? Not when we know that by unseeing the visible in consciousness and accepting the living Word as present, we are opening the door to the transmutation process which leads to eternal life. We are making a conscious choice, and let's go further than that. Let's search out all the divine commands given to us by Christ in scripture. Let's trust them, not by repeating them with our lips, but by rejecting every appearance that denies them. Make a practice of this. Accept what Christ says and at the same time un-accept the opposite.

If Christ says, "I am the life," that means I am the life of you. Do not accept another life. If Christ says, "I am the way," that means Christ is the way. Do not accept another way. If Christ says, "I am the door," do not walk through another door.

To accept the truth, to accept the divine command, is to reject that command which is not divine, that truth which is not divine. And as you practice this principle you will find you're in the principle of no power, and then you are saying to God, "I love *your* perfection. I accept *your* perfection. I accept your Kingdom on earth now. I accept you as the present Spirit of my being, and so I give power to no thing, place or person. I am faithful everyday to no power because *your* power is working, is present, is perfect. To your truth I open my Soul."

And you will know by the harmony that is restored into your daily life that the invisible wheels of transformation and transmutation are working to open the book of life for you, just as it has for all Souls who learn that the way to eternal life is to love God, the living Word in you, supremely.

LESSON 19: WORLD WORK: ENERGY

Our nineteenth lesson is very special because it is a group meditation for the next month starting now on energy. We are going to apply the principle of no power. Before the meditation it would be wise for you to consider first: "What is the truth?"

The human condition is that we are lacking an energy source which is adequate for our needs. It is not only a localized national lack but an international lack. Of course, to us it is evidence that man is again separated from the Kingdom of God. There's no energy crisis in the creation of God. There's no limit of energy in infinite God. And therefore the condition which does not exist in the creation of God only exists in the world of man because the human mind of man has not found a way to be a transparency to the reality.

Man is looking for energy from science, from inventors, from human material processes, from things, from the bowels of the physical earth and from the solar system. He's wracked his brain to find energy. He doesn't see the paradox that much of the energy that he wants is to be used to kill. As a matter of fact, perhaps science does know that it is useless to appeal to God for energy. Certainly, science never consults God and says, "Where can we find more energy?"

But it should be clear to all of us that you're not going to get energy from God to use for the purpose of breaking the commandment "Thou shalt not kill." We need energy to send our missiles to an enemy and knock them out of civilization. We need energy to send our warships and our planes. Is that not a perversion of energy? We need industry, not only for production of vital necessary goods, but to give us new energy so that we can continue to live in *this* world. We're not looking for energy to lift us *out* of this world, and so there is a vast chasm between God and man.

Man is not listening to God. Man is not listening to the Word. Man is not turning within and saying, "Father what is *your* will? Give us this energy; that's what we want. Well, our meditation is quite different. We are seeking divine energy, not physical energy, not human energy. We are saying that energy is present now. The infinite storehouse of God is present now with all the energy that man will ever need. It will filter through to the degree that it will be used only for God's purpose, no other.

Now you're not going to change that, and I'm not going to change that, because that's the way it is. Divine energy can only be used for divine purpose, and divine energy is the only energy there is. And for that divine energy to overflow into our life we must together be a transparency for the living Word. And so at 8 p.m. California time all of us who are dedicated to loving God supremely will join in a group awareness of the nature of God, the nature of energy and the nature of no power.

We'll do it now together getting the feel of it, the confidence that we are not appealing to God. We are not seeking God power. We are accepting that God has already provided all that is necessary. And how that energy manifests in our lives is not ours to decide or to anticipate or to predetermine.

"I of mine own self can do nothing, but the Father within, He doeth the works." I'm not asking for more coal or more sun power or more moon power or more star power or more atomic power. I am asking for nothing. I am resting in the living Word which doeth the works and accepting its living presence and power, for I have transcended the material sense of energy. We are standing together in the one infinite Soul, open to truth, receiving truth invisible.

Thank You, Father, for the ever presence and the everywhere presence of your divine energy. I feel it all around me. It is here. It is energizing your complete universe. It is the life-blood of creation. There is no shortage of it. It is now. It is the energy of divine love, the energy of divine will, the energy of divine life.

How could there be a shortage? I have turned it away. I have shut myself from it. I have denied its presence. I have been greedy. I have said, "Put this energy to use on this project and that project. I have not said, "Put it to use only on God's project." I have divided myself from that energy, I and the rest of my human brothers.

But in our Soul we have no human desire. We have no human need. We are outside that sense of body called human. We are in the mystical body, which is completely activated by the energy of God. We are in the infinite laboratory of source where all energy begins and where energy is eternal. This is how we meditate, and we must remain here for the realization.

The secret of realization is that the truth in consciousness understood, received in the Soul after we have transcended mind, will now flow through our transparent capacity, transforming us in consciousness into the awareness of energy, the conscious knowledge of energy without our doing anything about it. This wisdom will flow.

And as it flows, when there is a realization that it is present, this energy will then overflow transmuting the blockades and obstacles and bottlenecks of the human world of lack into abundance of energy. And it will flow in its own quantity, in it own measure, in its own direction without human intervention. And it will power the machines that should be powered. And it will power the lives that are walking in their Soul. And it will power the peace that men have been seeking and the harmony and the abundance and the life without end. Eternal energy received in your Soul will transmute this world into the Kingdom of God. It will dissolve the veil of ignorance that separates man from the treasures of the infinite Kingdom. Ye shall know this truth, and this truth will reveal living energy for your community, your nation, your universe. That will be the nature of our meditation.

Divine energy is present, and no power can limit it or deflect it. The seven T.R.'s are at work wherever there is a willing consciousness to be a receiver of the Word. Son, all My energy is thine. All that I have is flowing infinitely where you are. It will come to you in many new ways. For it is a divine law that all that the Father has the Son has, and we are now the Son of God.

Our invisible supply of energy is now present. The conditioned mind of man is the separation. We are transcending that conditioned mind. We are transcending the limitations which are imposed upon man by that conditioned mind. We are one with Source. We are thanking the Father for His living presence. We are accepting identity as the living Spirit of the Father, and we are in that consciousness which reveals that the power, presence, grace, love, justice and abundance of the Father is ever present, for I am with you always. Be still in that glorious knowledge every night, and let us transform what man calls an energy crisis into an invisible transmutation that reveals that energy is God. God is energy. They are one, and that One I Am.

We'll be together, then, in this as a group; and it is all part of our preparation for that unconditioned consciousness which is a pure transparency for divine law.

Your love is felt here in Kauai, and be sure that it is reciprocated. We are all held together in the bonds of divine love, one eternal self. Until we meet soon, probably tonight, Aloha from Kauai.

TAPE 6

LESSONS 20 - 22

Herb: From the island of Kauai, once more we bring you a message of Love.

In just a little under a month we shall be gathered together in the inn at Avila Beach, there to find our way into the Universe of God that lies outside of time. We have been preparing together for this event for some eight months now this year, studying the mystical idea that permeates the Bible, which was placed there for the purpose of leading us into the Kingdom of God on earth. And this tape, our sixth tape, will be the final tape before that seminar rather than the original seven tapes planned. You might consider that the first class of the seminar will be the seventh tape.

And so today, as we begin our twentieth lesson, it is very necessary that we all come to several points of agreement so that we can enter the seminar in a group consciousness so uplifted, so ready for the living Word, that we do not have to retrace our steps and banish concepts that might act as some sort of an opacity.

LESSON 20: TAKING THE CHRIST OFF THE CROSS

Today in particular we want to open the Bible. We want to remedy the neglect of centuries that has caused mankind to look at his Bible with unseeing eyes. The blame, if any, is placed directly upon the world mind, which in our contemporary society appears in

132

many forms such as religion, science, philosophy, education, and in all of the various walks of life where men and women seek truth but find it not.

I think without condemnation it is true to say that religion in the main has been a failure. It has not produced the Kingdom of God, and it has not produced peace on earth because it has not produced the living Word of God. I need not underline that all around us the distress of our world is a clear indication that the message of God has not yet reached the heart of mankind. It has been obstructed by a great deal of human will and so-called human intelligence, so much so that the message of Christ, the message that God sent to you and to me, is still a seed waiting to be germinated within us.

We have said that the guide for our journey from sense to Soul is truth and that only with the truth can we enter into that glorious transformation, which in turn leads to a transmutation and finally leads to eternal life, the transition from this world of form and matter into the permanent universe of pure Spirit.

This truth we find available to us in two ways: From the words of the prophets endowed by the Father with the wisdom of God, and directly within ourselves from the Father if we are attuned to the Infinite. Our Bible, for the purpose of developing this capacity to live only in truth, contains much that still is unknown to the minds of men.

One such passage, which today must be explored with a great deal of vigor and intensity, is found in Luke one, the thirty-fifth verse. The angel Gabriel has announced to Mary the very special manner in which she will conceive a child named Jesus. She's been prepared for this all her life, just like her mother before her. And though she is only a child you might say, not yet fourteen years old, this holy visitation comes upon her; and she wants to know how will it be that she can conceive without a man. The angel says, "The Holy Ghost shall come upon thee, and...overshadow thee:

and therefore...to that holy thing which shall be born of thee shall be called the Son of God."

Now those are the words that we want to concentrate upon: "that holy thing which shall be born of thee will be called the Son of God." Up to now those words have a false meaning for most of mankind. The teaching given by religion is that the Son of God is Jesus Christ; that Jesus Christ is the only Son; that before Jesus there was no Son; that after Jesus there is no Son. And so the total concentrated effort of religion has been to place absolute emphasis on the fact that this one, Jesus, is the son born to Mary; and this son, this person, this holy person, is the one you and I are to follow in order to fulfill God's purpose for us.

Now this is the largest, most immense half truth or quarter truth or one-eighth truth ever presented in the world by religion. It is so far from the mark that it has led mankind astray. It is the false beginning, and from it has come a false foundation; and on that false foundation has been erected an edifice of untruth so unlike the teaching of Jesus Christ, so unlike the will and purpose of God, that day by day, year by year, century by century, mankind has strayed farther and farther away from truth. He has become a prodigal in the sense that he does not know the Son of God, and inasmuch as only the Son of God knows the Father, mankind is separated from the Father; and in this separation you will find the cause of every human problem on this earth.

The Son of God is the focal point where we can undo, unlearn the tremendous error perpetrated by many men of dedication and sincerity who simply have never been able to read the mystical code of God in their hearts or in their Bible. Today we must take Christ off the cross where he has been placed by the religious mind of this world.

Before we put our attention to the task of understanding the importance of the Son of God in our life, I want you to see just how much *you* are prepared to make this great advance in your understanding. You are no longer a neophyte. Through The

Infinite Way you have been privileged to dwell with the saints in a message of truth that knows no superior on this earth. You've come quite a distance from your earliest days in orthodoxy. You have traveled through metaphysics, and you have opened the book of mysticism, which is direct contact with the Father within. And you may judge exactly or to some degree where you are in consciousness simply by listening to a few simple questions and asking yourself how they relate to your present awareness.

For example: What is an old Soul? What does that mean to you? Are you one? Are the people in this world around you old Souls to you? Do you accept them as pre-existent to this form? Do you accept that they have been here many times before in other forms and that they are part of an ongoing up-going learning process? Have you accepted your permanent name? Do you know what it is? Do you still believe that you are flesh that dies? Do you believe that divine life can enter the physical womb of a woman?

Do you worship truth? Do you worship God at the Soul level instead of the mind level? Can you see without eyes? Can you hear without ears? Which do you put first, your will or the will of God? Are you ready, willing, unafraid to live your divine life now? Do you hate the life you have in this world or do you love it? And think carefully about that question. What does Christ consciousness mean to you? Do you think that it is possible for you to live now in the Kingdom of God on earth even while you appear in this world?

Now our study so far has prepared us so that questions of this nature are not what you might call shocking or surprising. We can feel at home with them. And so with that preparation, with that level of awareness, we want to look now at what might be called the immaculate misconception. We want to discover why religion has misconceived the most glorious teaching in the world, and above all we want to discover what mankind has overlooked.

And we say to ourselves, "Well then, who is this Son of God?" Is it not Jesus as religion has defined it? And the answer is no, it is not Jesus as religion has defined it. As religion has given the message of the Son of God to man, we have a message which completely buries the truth about the identity of the Son of God. And the repercussions of that message, of that error, are almost tantamount to heresy, because in so doing, religion has actually torn up the New Testament and repudiated the Old Testament and has substituted an impotent, totally ineffectual group of human rules, which are so devoid of spiritual content that the power of God has been denied to the human race by the very individuals who think they are opening out a way for man to enter into salvation.

Now the one and only Son of God, it should be clear to you and to me and ultimately to our neighbor, is not Jesus Christ. Nor would Jesus Christ have it that way, because we have many incidents in the Bible speaking about the Son of God and the Sons of God long before Jesus. And to teach that Jesus Christ is the Son we must wait for; to teach that the Son of God was betrayed, humiliated, spat upon, crucified, buried, resurrected, and then departed to give us all a chance to repent, this superficial blaspheming type of concept about the infinite Son of God must be met by you and me in our consciousness in such a way that the identity of that Son is unveiled, not just as a––well, as an observation or as a belief that we are told we should share––but as an experience within our own consciousness; and I will say much more about that experience.

If we take a look at our Bible again, we find that we are given thousands of clues on every page to tell us that the Son of God is not a person, not a man of flesh or a woman of flesh, not a form. And if we only look first at a few passages to see that "Son of God" is not an idea that began with Jesus, we would at least shatter this old concept which has shackled mankind into a denial of the holy truth that can liberate mankind from its tomb of ignorance.

We can look at Daniel. There is in the third chapter, the twenty-fifth verse, this statement: We have Nebuchadnezzar seeing these three men in the furnace, and he looks, and behold there are four instead of the three, and he says, "...I see four men loose, walking in the midst of the fire, and they have no hurt; and the form of the fourth is like the Son of God." The Son of God. Why did he name the fourth as like the Son of God? There was no Jesus on the earth.

We look into Job, the 38th chapter, the seventh verse; and he says, "When the morning stars sang together, and all the Sons of God shouted for joy?" Men were very conscious of the Sons of God going back to antiquity. That was before Jesus. And what about after? What about you? What about four billion? What about us?

The truth now is this: The immaculate conception of Jesus Christ gives us an inner teaching which includes hundreds of secrets. And among these hundreds of secrets are solutions that can remove from this earth every problem that man has been unable to solve. The entire mystery of man and the universe is contained for us in the immaculate conception. And, above and beyond all the many secrets divulged there, is the chief one, *teaching how you and I as individuals can release the full power of God into our daily experience.* And it is now time for us to end forever the human persecution of Christ. Together we take Christ down from the cross. For as long as Christ remains crucified in your mind, in the mind of mankind, in the mind of religion, it is you and I who are being hung, not Christ.

Let's look again at the immaculate conception, and let us break through the crust of centuries, break through the errors that have dragged the human race down into their graves. Mankind has never seen the Son of God, even when Jesus walked the streets. They saw Jesus, but they did not see the Son of God.

The Son of God is the invisible life of God. The Son of God was not the infant body of Jesus. The Son of God was not in the womb of Mary. The Son of God did not live inside the body of Jesus. The Son of God is entirely different than it has been portrayed to mankind. It was portrayed correctly by Jesus Christ and then misconceived by the so-called holy hierarchies of this world.

The true Son cannot act independent of God; there is no way. The true Son cannot think independent of God, and that is because the Son is the life of God. The life of the Son of God is the very same life that is God, and so the Son of God can never die because the life of God can never die. The Son of God can never be crucified because the life of God can never be crucified, and that life remains perfect forever. And so the Son lives in perfection forever. The son never lives in a temporary lifespan. The Son of God, the life of God, never lives in a form of flesh. The life of God is never influenced by the illusions of the senses. The life of God is infinite and the Son of God is infinite life, totally independent of all of the finite forms, material powers and material laws of this world.

Please remember the Son of God is not a person, not a physical child born of a woman, and that divine life never lives in a temporary body or in a temporary lifespan. Now if we can go that far together we are making strides, and these are going to lead to the understanding of who the Son of God is, where the Son of God is and how the Son of God functions.

You see, God was not revealing one special birth at the immaculate conception. God was revealing what eyes could not see, as if God was saying, *"I am making clear to you this secret, that human birth is not what your eyes see; it is something else. I am making the invisible visible. I am opening your own inner eye to the truth that you were immaculately conceived as the life of God before your parents and their parents appeared on earth. And that your life was the life of God even before this world appeared in time and is the life of God now and forever. The immaculate conception is a universal immaculate conception revealing that the life of God is the invisible life of the human race."*

Now with that in mind, we go directly to the Christ which appeared to us in our consciousness in the form of Jesus. We

138

are looking for the truth that the Father placed in the Son, not for human truth; and we find it through the words of Jesus. Specifically, Christ, the invisible life which appears to us as Jesus, says to us, *"I am the life."* Meaning, I am the life of God. *"I am not the life of a human form, but I am the invisible life, the life that you do not see. The life of this child called Jesus, I am the invisible life of this child, but I am infinite. I am the invisible life of every child. I am the invisible life of you and your so-called children and parents. I am the invisible life of Mary as well as Jesus. I am the invisible life of the disciples of Jesus. I am the invisible life of Buddha and Krishna and Lao-tsu. I am the life of all, for there is no other life. And I am the way, and I am the truth. There is no other truth."*

The moment you have another life than I, the invisible life, you have lost the Son of God. The Son of God should never be personalized, for the Son of God is life, the life of God. *"I, the invisible life, am the way, the truth; and no man cometh to the Father but by me."*

Now it should be clear, then, that the Son of God, the immaculate conception of the Son of God is the birth in your consciousness that you are that Son of God. That is the immaculate conception. When you through inner experience realize that you are the Son of God, the life of God, that is your immaculate conception.

Now to make sure that you know all this, the life of God says, through Jesus, "Thou seest me." Meaning, when you see Jesus, you are really seeing life. "Thou seest me, thou seest the Father." He is revealing the invisible life of God where he stands, "for I and the Father," I and the life, "are one." One invisible life stands here.

And then comes a new idea, an idea that was not possible until we had traveled this far. "He that hateth his life in this world shall keep it unto life eternal." He has revealed his invisible life is God, infinite life, and now tells you to hate your life in this world. Why would he say this? Except to show there is a difference between your life and the life of God. That your human life is not the life of

God, and so you are to hate your life in this world. He is drawing a distinction between your life as a human and your life as the Son of God. He is showing you that you have another life than the one you think you're living. And some of us have already made inroads into this type of passover or crossing over.

The life of your human form is not the life of God. You're going to have to face that. And the glory is that before we learned the mystical truth we only had our human life, and now we see that the human life that fades, disappears, dies, is not our life at all. In our immaculate conception, in the birth of Christ in consciousness, we are told to step out of our human sense of life, not accept it. That is hating your life in this world. And, instead, "He that loveth his life in this world shall lose it."

Isn't that exactly what the human race is doing? Isn't that what most of us have done most of our human lives, loving our life in this world? And that's because we knew of no other life. We had not learned that the Son of God is our own divine life. And then when we know our name; when we know that the name of our divine life is "I"; when we can say "I," meaning my divine life, then you can understand why the Christ again says, "I shall give you the keys to the Kingdom." Of course, because the moment you know that divine life is your name; that you are I, the Life of God, the Son of God, you have the keys to the Kingdom.

And so remember this: Whenever you see the form of Jesus in the Bible––Jesus going into Capernum or Jesus sailing across the Sea of Galilee or Jesus coming to do another miraculous healing, Jesus going and coming––you're not seeing Jesus. You only think you are. You're really seeing the Father, the invisible life of God. And so we're going to call Jesus that outer form, that symbol in the mind of man which we see when we look at the invisible life of God. And then when you see the powers of Jesus, you're always seeing the powers of the invisible life of God.

"Of myself, I can do nothing. The Father within, he doeth the works."

But remember, the visible life is not the Son. Only the invisible life is the Son, and only the invisible life gives you the keys. Now where are you in this picture? The life of God said, "Do not put new wine in old bottles." In metaphysics, we sopped up truth. We were the old bottles, and we were trying to find the new wine; and we put it into the old human self, the old human brain, the old human body.

In mysticism, we do not make this error. The new wine bottle for the new wine is the Son of God. The life of God is your new wine bottle. And until you will accept the life of God as your life, you are putting new wine in old bottles; and you will lose it.

"Take off your shoes." Remove your connection to this earth. Step out of your earthbound shoes. Step out of your human beliefs, your material concepts, your material sense of life. You are now infinite being, infinite life; and unless you accept the qualities of infinite life as your qualities you are not taking off your shoes.

So many people have been saying, "I believe in Jesus." But they do not believe in the Son of God other than Jesus, and this is precisely why the life of God says, through Jesus, "Why call ye me Lord, Lord and do not the things which I say?" Ever mankind is being reminded that it is not enough to accept a savior in the form of a man. It doesn't matter which one you follow. If you do not accept the true savior––the life of God––as your life, but continue in the sense of a life in form, a life that ages, a life that is subject to the ills of the flesh, you are just saying Lord, Lord, but you are not doing what the Lord says.

Paul was very firm about this. "Be not deceived. God is not mocked. For whatever a man soweth, that shall he also reap. For he that soweth to the flesh shall of the flesh reap corruption."

He was not speaking about lust. He was not speaking about what we call human sin. He was not even speaking of the various things that preachers threaten mankind with if they are unable to break the chains of desire, ambition, and that whole parade of human good and evil. But when he spoke of sowing to the flesh, he was speaking of accepting yourself as human life, accepting a life in form as your life. That is sowing to the flesh in its true sense.

Instead, says Paul, "He that soweth to the Spirit shall of the Spirit reap life everlasting." And the Spirit is the life of God in you. It only remained now for John to remind us that the invisible life of Jesus Christ, which was the life of God, was also the invisible life of all men. And that that life is here now, and that life is the Kingdom of God.

Let us be still a moment. Let us rest in our divine life, feeling the truth of it.

I am life itself. My life is not the life of this human form. I am not fooled into accepting a dying life. I accept my own immaculate conception. I accept the Word of God. My name, though I speak it not to men, is inscribed in my heart. I am forever the Son of God. The invisible life of God is my life forever. It is the only life that I have. It is not in the future. It is not something I will earn. It is what I am.

The secret splendor of the life of God is released within my consciousness as I accept it, as I accept the Will which that life expresses and remove all human sense of will which is born of a human sense of life and accept all qualities of that divine life as my qualities without opposite.

And with this knowledge I strengthen and reaffirm my capacity to endure anything, any test, any condition with the sure knowledge that the life of God is my life and the life of all, and is free of all conditions that may appear in this world. This capacity, when developed with faith, courage, intensity, opens the gates of heaven on earth; and then we are led to the true, the real, the immaculate conception that has been missed by the religions of the world.

When you have proven your obedience to the will of the life of God in you, only then does that life yield to you the keys to the Kingdom. No Soul can live in the Kingdom until it takes dominion over human will. And when this dominion is established, human will no longer governs the form or the life of the form. World powers then appear as illusion. The concept of flesh is subdued and dissolved. The mortal dream is shattered. You move beyond sickness, beyond death, out of a temporary lifespan, no longer living in a human body or in a material world; but you still remain visible. This is the liberated consciousness, and in this state of consciousness it is revealed to you as a living experience that the invisible life of God is your life and that you are the Son of God.

Many Souls on earth have attained this inner experience. It is the supreme achievement, the fulfillment of your search for God; and with it, your transition will be the passing over from human sense of life into divine life realized. This is your realization of oneness.

∞∞∞∞∞∞∞∞∞ End of Side One ∞∞∞∞∞∞∞∞∞

You may have noticed one important fact that now must be stressed: The life of every human form is separated from God. When you look over the world of men, you are looking at forms living a sense of life that is separated from God. The life of the form that dies when the form dies is not the life of God that lives forever, and it is this separation between form and the real life which must be overcome.

Wherever form and the real life are joined in one, you will see the powers of God made visible. Wherever an individual accepts the immaculate conception in consciousness and goes through the experience of being the life of God again and again and again until all is welded into one consciousness called life consciousness, Son of God consciousness. When that happens, you too will sing with the morning star.

One universal life. One universal immaculate conception. Take it away from one man on this earth, and you have taken it away from yourself. For in divine life there is never any division.

LESSONS 21- 22: REVEALING THE SEVEN STEPS

In the last lesson among the things we learned is that the human form and the human life are separated from the life of God, and therefore the power of the life of God does not enter into human experience until this is remedied. And so when you discover that your life is barren in some areas, whatever those areas might be, you're really unaware of it at the time, but what you are missing is your own awareness that you are the life of God; and you may try to remedy this with your mind. You may say to yourself ten times, "I am the life of God." And for some reason, the power of that life does not express. It doesn't come forth as supply or employment or a happy marriage or a child who recovers from some kind of an ailment. And you say, "Well, I thought it worked; if I'm the life of God, it's got to be better."

And that is where your mystical training comes in. You see, the life of God is functioning and your five senses are denying that you are the life of God. Your five senses are saying, "I have no supply." And the life of God is saying, "I am supply." And you're saying, "Well, go ahead and show some of it." And the life of God says, "I can't. I can only express it through My own life. My own life has no supply and the you that has no supply is not there. I can't express through nothing."

Now whenever you find a lack or limitation or an appearance of disease or disaster, it is there because you are not living as the life of God. You are living as the life of a human form. And if you do that from now till the day when you disappear from this earth without making a change, do not expect the power of the life of God to function through you. You must unite your form with the life of God in your consciousness.

You must accept the life of God as having no opposite. You must hate your life in this world. You must recognize that you have no life in this world. And you must learn the technique which enables you to do this, because without this truth growing in consciousness, you will not be one with the transmutation process which takes you into the experience of transition.

We learn to look at all false appearances with the knowledge that they are not part of the life of God, and therefore they are not part of me; and therefore no matter what they present, they are the tempter; and my function is to say, "I, being the life of God, can look at these temptations to say that I am not the life of God and realize that they are not part of my being."

I may have to do this for the next hour or for the next year, but I've got to do it. I've got to do it so that every temptation is met with the knowledge that this condition does not exist in the life of God. That is the only way I can accept the life of God.

The seven T.R.'s on the fifth tape are the divine plan to lift you and mankind out of the wheel of mortality into divine life. All intelligent God-seeking men and women before us have labored for centuries to find the Kingdom of eternal life, but they have failed in many cases because they have tried to think their way into heaven.

The seven T.R.'s are the secret path of no thought. The plan is independent of you. You either make yourself available to it or you don't, but its working does not depend on you. It is always working. The only way you can enter that plan is with your shoes off––that is, by submitting your entire being on the altar of truth, and truth alone, until you yourself become the eternal flame and the substance of the flame; and all that is not the flame is burned away.

Your transmutation in consciousness from human body to eternal mystical body, from human life to eternal divine life, fulfills the mission of your Soul. This is called your initiation of earth. Every Soul must pass through it on its return journey to the full stature of divine individuality. To reveal this seven-pronged process to all dedicated Souls has been the purpose of this mystical series––to unite you into oneness with the infinite divine force.

And as this happens you will fully realize why Jesus said, "I of mine own self can do nothing."

In your physical sense of body there is an automatic process that circulates your blood. It regulates your heartbeat. It digests your food. It happens independent of you. These processes of the body are not waiting for your mind to direct them consciously. They're automatic. They function without your conscious thought. But remember, these bodily processes also break down, and they break down because they are separated from the life of God. All human body processes are merely copies. They are counterfeit copies of the perfect divine processes that now are taking place in your mystical body in your divine life.

We all know about Moses, but what we do not seem to realize is that he introduced his mystical body to mankind; and there was no method of communicating the divine idea to the mind of the struggling human race at that time. The Hebrews at that time and the world today do not recognize that the hidden manna falling from the sky was an invisible process in the mystical body of Moses, and it was working just as automatically as circulation, breathing, digestion and heartbeats work in our human body.

The human mind believed that the hidden manna produced by Moses in the wilderness, and later the barley loaves multiplied by Elijah, were a very special dispensation from God. But they were wrong. It was actually a spiritual principle being demonstrated, a universal unfailing principle which is part of the divine plan for all mankind. Moses and Elijah had discovered the principle of automatic transmutation, and they had opened the book of life walking through the secret path of transformation into their mystical body, which automatically transmutes its own divine substance to meet every need without human thought.

It was because of this invisible mystical body that Moses could seem to die at the age of one hundred and twenty and yet reappear in a conversation with Jesus fifteen hundred years later.

Similarly, just as your human body transmutes food into energy, blood, bone and muscle, your invisible mystical body transmutes life into spiritual energy, power, fulfillment, harmony, peace; and these divine qualities overflow into your visible life automatically as the fulfillment of every earthly need. That's what you saw in all the miraculous healings of Jesus Christ. They were performed to demonstrate the automatic principle of transmutation.

"I will, be thou cleansed. Stretch forth thine arm. Arise, take up thy bed and walk." But instead, the world worshipped the man Jesus. They marveled at his so-called divine powers. They memorized his inspired words. They honored him with statues and with churches, and they continued to ignore the principle of transmutation which he taught as the cornerstone of the new life for all mankind, not just for one.

That one principle is still a mystery to mankind because it was not described openly in the Bible, and because those who had no eyes to see it never brought it to the attention of those who could not see it in the Bible, and because man has continued to accept a mortal body and a temporary lifespan. We have not seen the activity of transmutation because we have not accepted our divine life. We have not accepted ourselves to be the life of God, the Son of God.

Now when we saw Jesus walking through the Holy Land, we should have observed that he left this clue when he also repeated the transmutation miracles of Moses and Elijah. The first time he multiplied five loaves and two fishes, that's the number seven, the key of transmutation. That is why the numbers five and two were used. They total seven, and seven means transmutation. He was saying, "As I start with seven and can feed five thousand, this same principle of transmutation can take man out of all the evil and death that this world knows into perfect eternal life."

You remember when he was asked to repeat this miracle? He cried out with dismay, "You want the loaves and the fishes, but you are overlooking the principle." Nevertheless, he did repeat the miracle; and the second time he multiplied loaves and fishes to emphasize the why and the how of breaking material law. This time he used seven fishes to feed four thousand people, and when they had finished this time there still remained seven baskets full.

He was teaching that transmutation to your mystical body, to your divine life in that mystical body, is the divine plan, is the path of transition, is the key to survival and salvation, is the secret method by which your Soul passes over the threshold of this the fourth world, the time world, and proceeds upward beyond mortal separation into unity with the Infinite. This is really the hidden meaning of the Hebrew Passover.

You see, David was the seventh son. Enoch was the seventh from Adam. In seven months Noah's ark rested on dry land. Jesus sent out seventy disciples. John saw seven stars, seven candlesticks, seven angels; and he sent seven letters to seven churches. Jesus taught us to forgive seventy times seven. The blind man recovered his vision on the seventh day, the Sabbath. God rested from his labors on the seventh day.

Do you see from cover to cover the Bible is sprinkled with sevens in combinations of seven to teach the great secret that man of earth must transmute to Son of God, that mortality must transmute to immortality, and that this transmutation must be total, not partial, total. For without total transmutation the separation from God will continue.

If we are listening, to the human race the Spirit of God, the Spirit of Love, is ever saying:

"Stop drifting into old age. Stop fearing. Stop suffering. Stop wondering about your future security and your health. Stop worrying about germs, radioactive atoms, inflation, recession, employment, armies going to war. And above all, stop the decaying, dying process of your body. Do what man has deemed impossible, which is not impossible to the Son of God. In the face of all the personal problems and universal problems of this world there is a practical path for you that surmounts every obstacle, and this path has been prepared

to restore you to your perfection. Don't grow old; transmute. Don't suffer; transmute. Don't die; transmute. You've been given the power to let the Spirit of God, which raised many Souls from the tomb of mortality, quicken your mortal body into eternal life. That quickening from dying flesh to the eternal light of your own pure being is the secret path of transmutation."

The Bible calls it by another name. The Bible calls it the descent of the Holy Ghost when radiant light replaces the creature born of the dust of earth. When Christ is born in your consciousness as the living presence of God and you accept this for every person, for every condition, then the Spirit of Love says, *"Be ye perfect. Ye are the light. You are not the changing creature. You are the divine child of God now, not an aging, suffering, separated, dying mortal."*

You are transmuted from human life, human form, to divine life in your mystical body of light.

"I, the life of God, accepted, I transmute your body. I, the life of God, accepted, I transmute your substance. I transmute your nature. I transmute your beliefs. I transmute your mind. I transmute your ways. I transmute your life. For I am the Spirit of Life, and I take you into your permanent selfhood which dwells now and forever in the finished Kingdom of God."

This transmutation in your consciousness is the sacred inner process ordained by Spirit for the eternal life and salvation of man. While you appear on this earth you will never have a more deeply moving experience than inner transmutation. Everything you have felt or known in your earth consciousness, no matter how exciting or how transcendental, will appear to be only a passing sensation compared to the indescribable all-consuming blackout of total transmutation.

The world moves away. Your identity diminishes to zero, and yet another you seems to be watching the deep sleep of the old you. Part of you seems dead, maybe all of you; but strangely there is a new life feeling. You find yourself being pulled on one hand into quicksand out of the world. Your life force in this world comes to an almost total standstill. Not only is your body without motion or emotion, it isn't there. And your thought process moves into an infinite silence, a strange absolute stillness as if every previous meditation had now merged into one infinite meditation, one overpowering eternal silence.

And yet this is only the first labor pain of your rebirth. When it is finished, you will know you are living in your mystical body. You will know that divine law governs everything you do until transition and after transition. This experience cannot come to you as long as you cling to the human sense of life.

We are going to pursue this in the explorations outside time, but something says to me that if we are to meet in one consciousness, it would be very good at this present moment to return to earthly things to clarify that we who strive to live in the invisible Kingdom of God are not unaware of what you may term earthly responsibilities. What we are aware of is that there is a way of fulfilling earthly responsibilities without breaking your fidelity to Spirit. And perhaps we might say that every time you accept any limitation or any sickness or any real so-called problem, you are really denying that you are the life of God. And so try to get the technique of turning this around, or as the Greek word is metanoia, change of mind––turn ye and live.

When you accept a problem, you are accepting another creator. You're really saying, "There's another creator besides God, because look at this problem." And so you're really playing right into the old-fashioned Satan idea. You've got some kind of second creator, or devil; and there isn't any. Every time you accept a problem, you are denying yourself to be the Son of God. And you can't deny it by accepting the problem and accept the powers of the Son of God to function. And so, "get thee behind me Satan" is necessary in order to accept divine Sonship.

God is the creator of all. God is not the creator of problems. I, the Son of God, do not have a problem even while the hurricane is bursting at the window or the airplane is spinning out of the sky or the flood is rising over the banks of the shore. I, the Son of God, do not have a problem. And it doesn't matter if it's a mosquito or something in your soup at the restaurant, or whatever it might be. I mean it can be minor or major. I, the Son of God, do not have a problem.

God says, *"There is no darkness in My life."* The life of God is too pure to behold iniquity. We cannot go around contradicting the Word of God. We cannot go around violating that I am the life of God, and we cannot deny that the power of the life of God is functioning. We must remember that power is functioning invisibly until you have accepted it without any form of equivocation and without any exceptions of any kind. Wherever you deny the activity of the power of God because you cannot see it, you are also denying the presence of God because you cannot see God. Where God is present, the power of God is functioning. And when you deny the presence of the power, you deny the presence of the presence; and you are denying the life of God as your life.

What are you doing it with? You're doing it with a second mind. You're not in oneness with the life because you're in a different mind than the mind of God, aren't you? You're not in the Christ mind. You're in a human mind, a sense mind; and there's your problem. The sense mind denies the presence and the power of the life of God. The sense mind presents and accepts the problem. And that sense mind is really within the world mind, and you are being treated like an atomic robot. You're nothing but a puppet in the world mind, which uses your sense mind to present what is not there, making it all so real to you.

"I haven't any supply." Neither did those in the wilderness who had only two and five loaves and fishes. "Well, Jesus isn't here to do it for me." "No, but Christ is." The principle of Christ in you, as the Life of you, is the principle that Jesus taught in the wilderness. But before you can accept it, you're going to have to sacrifice your tremendous brain-power, which is so superior to the Word of God.

When you sacrifice your brain-power and accept that the mind of God knows more than your brain, and surrender to the mind of God, the life of God, and accept the mind of God as your mind, the consciousness of God as your consciousness, because the consciousness of the life of God is also your consciousness, then you can say to your human mind, "Be still."

And even though your human mind can't see through the problem, your fidelity to the knowledge that you are the life of God is your only offense and defense. That's how you get out of being an image accepting images and stop making God the creator of this world; stop accepting your temporary sense of body, your temporary sense of conditions, your temporary sense of life, your temporary sense of flesh; stop accepting sickness, pain, fear and dying as part of real creation. As you face these human issues with that one consciousness, you are standing fast; and you will behold the salvation of the Lord within yourself.

We are soon going to meet, and the messages will be taped, of course, so that those of you who are not able to come can join the spiritual feast with us. And it seems right at this time to join in the acceptance of one life. Never my life or his life or her life, but one universal divine life without opposite. We're standing above the world illusion, and an angel from God is entering our consciousness to announce the glorious news that we shall be overshadowed, that our mind shall no longer hold sway, that we can with total peace surrender to our own divine life.

"Be thou perfect as thy Father."

While you walk this earth accept your invisible perfection. Live in your own invisibility; and your visible world will be transformed. The Son of God will walk this earth where you appear to be, and that Son of God will be your permanent Self.

Bring the blessing of your divine consciousness to the seminar, and what you take home with you will be beyond all human expectations. Love is the prevailing feeling at this moment. A love of the truth of God, a love of the truth that we can share as one, a love of where we are going and why, a love of all that God is. With that Love we say "Aloha" until we meet at Avila Beach to shake hands, to look at each other with eyes that see the reality where the world sees only the form.

See you very soon.

The End